WINE TOURS
IN THE
SOUTH OF FRANCE

For Noéline, my daughter, my little star, and the sunshine of my life,
who was born the day after I submitted the manuscript for this book.
During my pregnancy she illuminated my path and my words from within.

FLORENCE HERNANDEZ

WINE TOURS
IN THE
SOUTH OF FRANCE

Flammarion

CONTENTS

FROM SUBTLE, CORAL-COLORED ROSÉS AND ROBUST,
FULL REDS TO PERFUMED, DRY WHITES AND SMOOTH
VINS DOUX NATURELS, THE WINES OF THE SOUTH OF
FRANCE ARE EXTRAORDINARILY DIVERSE, REFLECTING A
MOSAIC OF VARIED TERROIRS AND APPELLATIONS.
FOLLOWING DOUBLE PAGE:
THESE VINES IN THE CORBIÈRES, BETWEEN THE
VILLAGES OF LAPALME AND LA FRANQUI,
LIE CLOSE TO THE MEDITERRANEAN AND ARE
IMPREGNATED WITH THE SALTY SEA AIR AND THE
DISTINCTIVE FRAGRANCE OF THE GARRIGUE.

INTRODUCTION

For a long time known as *petits vins*, the wines of the South of France in fact have everything it takes to be great. There are magnificent grape varieties, eminent appellations, great wines, and world-famous names. It is almost as if, in these regions of sunshine and fine living, God himself inhabited these wines, using as his witnesses the little châteaux and squat houses, the vines and vineyards that are the major source of wealth on this impoverished land. But what do we expect of these wines? Perhaps that they should set the seal on a moment of shared pleasure and friendship and reveal to us the secrets of a *terroir* or a life. This book was written to escape from the world of superficial appearances and drinkers of labels, in a search for pleasure and conviviality. Writing it has enabled me to discover many exciting estates, some established and some up and coming, to see many magnificent settings and enjoy many unforgettable experiences and emotions. My aim is to present here only those wines that have the taste of true, authentic, and unpretentious winemaking, free from exaggerated reputations and media hype.

Thus, like a pilgrim of the vineyard, I wandered as my fancy took me, going from cellar to cellar, from Cahors to Madiran and from Châteauneuf-du-Pape to the Côtes-de-Provence, in search of a rare bouquet, exciting hints of future perfection, flavors that were unknown but subsequently revealed. I visited regions in which wine is not just a drink, but also a message. Here and there—that is to say, everywhere—a glass of wine can tell those not afraid of enjoying themselves about a whole culture and way of life. The people who tend these vineyards speak of both the temporal and spiritual heritage that they serve in all humility, but paradoxically with the right amount of irreverence, modernity, daring, and sincerity. And this apparent contradiction between respect for tradition and enthusiasm for the modern simply makes their wines all the more attractive.

Wine is the creation of desire.
RAYMOND DUMAY

We live in the era of the wine bar, of wine by the glass, of impudent bistros that offer novel combinations of food and wine, along with the chance to discover those "little wines." You might first taste these wines all by yourself, but you will be anxious to share them with your friends at the first opportunity. And travel, of course, must include some gourmet occasions and gastronomic detours—in other words, it has to include some of those unimpeachable addresses that provide a feast for the eyes and the taste buds, stamped with the seal of the finest local products from the soil and the vine. This kind of tourism in France has become an art and touring wine country has become a lifestyle experience. In visiting these extraordinary places, I have avoided where possible the beaten track. I have attempted to learn how to taste wine and to understand what makes regional wines typical. I have met people and listened to them, and I have bought the wines that best corresponded to my tastes and my budget. Americans, with their pioneering spirit, have been quick to understand what was happening to the vineyards in the southern half of France. They were among the first to visit these winemaking estates much as other people visit museums.

Wine lovers, whether they prefer the Old or New World styles, have long known that a good wine is not merely the fruit of the soil or the sun. It requires hard work, patience, rigor, and passion. The owners and estates that I describe here all have these qualities. The wonderful wines in these pages have been created in historic locations, by exceptional people. These are the criteria that have guided my choice, which is not in any way exhaustive. It remains, and will always remain, for enthusiasts to discover a new wine or a patch of vines capable of arousing their emotions, and such finds may never appear in a book, except perhaps for a record of the cellars visited.

This book therefore offers the finest offerings of the vine, and is to be read with a glass in hand. Now it is up to us to show ourselves worthy of them.

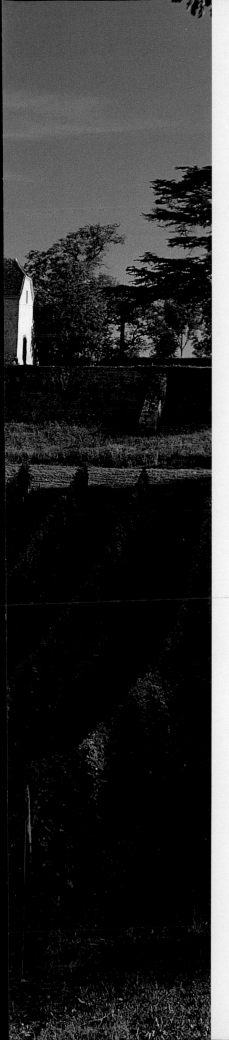

THE SOUTHWEST

Château de Crouseilles produces attractive,
harmonious reds with smooth tannins.

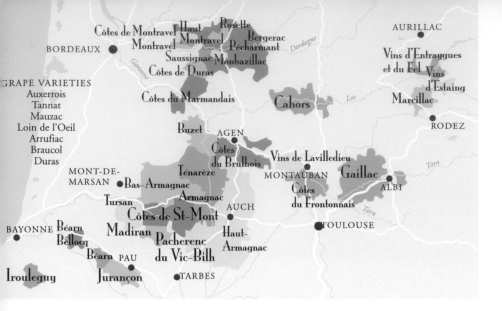

THE SOUTHWEST:
PERFECT HARMONY WITH THE CUISINE OF GASCONY

The wines of Cahors, Gaillac, Madiran, and Pacherenc de Vic-Bihl all grace our dinner tables from time to time, but the undervalued Côtes-de-Duras, Tursan, Jurançon, and Côtes-du-Frontonnais tend to be noticeable by their absence. Yet these appellations sometimes dismissed as lesser wines possess undeniable qualities. Their aromas are subtle and varied, they can age and mature wonderfully in the cellar, and they offer good value for money. Whether light and fruity or full-bodied and powerful, they are usually attractive wines that typify the Southwest. The vineyards cover an area of 173,000 acres (70,000 hectares), extending over four main regions and seven *départements*, namely the Pyrénées-Atlantiques, Landes, Lot-et-Garonne, Lot, Tarn, Tarn-et-Garonne, and Haute-Garonne.

This is a lovable region, a landscape of mountains and rolling hills, where French provincial cooking continues to attract hordes of visitors who have given up on worrying about their waistlines. From the shores of the Garonne to the valley of the Lot, through the Basque country, the Pyrenees, and Gascony, this mosaic of time-honored vineyards produces a variegated palette of *terroirs* and thus a diversity of exceptional wines. Nowhere else in France can you find such a large number of local varieties. West of Albi, in the Gaillac, you will find Braucol, Ondenc, and Mauzac; on the slopes of Marmandais there is Abouriou; in the Côtes du Frontonnais there is Négrette; and in Cahors the Bordeaux variety Malbec is used under the name of Auxerrois.

The Comité Interprofessionnel des Vins du Sud-Ouest was officially created in December 1997 and covers sixteen appellations from Aquitaine to the Midi-Pyrénées. There are also nine appellations (Béarn, Côtes-du-Frontonnais, Gaillac, Irouléguy, Jurançon, Madiran, Marcillac, Pacherenc du Vic-Bilh, and Floc de Gascogne) and seven VDQS (Vin Délimité de Qualité Supérieure) designations, namely Côtes-du-Brulhois, Côtes-de-Millau, Côtes-de-Saint-Mont, Estaing, Entraygues et Fel, Lavilledieu, and Tursan.

Although in the past you had to be Basque to truly appreciate the Irouléguy, this, the smallest appellation in the Southwest, has benefited in recent years from the rigor and expertise of talented winemakers. Today, shrewd wine buffs are happy to include these lively, strongly aromatic wines in their cellars, wines such as Domaines d'Ilarria, Domaine de Brana, and Domaine d'Arretxea. The red wines are powerful and long in the mouth, while the rosés are vivacious, luminous, and aromatic, making wonderful accompaniments to cured meats such as Bayonne ham, or other local specialties such as elvers, or poultry from the Landes.

The vines of Jurançon continue to produce extraordinary wines. The grapes grow in the Pyrenean foothills south of Pau, at an altitude of one thousand feet (three hundred meters). This nectar of kings and king of nectars was discovered by Henri IV at his baptism. The land is divided into little terraces that cascade down into sunlit valleys, where the

THE RED WINES OF THE SOUTHWEST HAVE BODY AND SPIRIT, AS TYPIFIED BY THE WINES OF CÔTES DE SAINT-MONT.
THESE ARE DARK AND FULL-BODIED, WITH AROMAS INITIALLY OF RED BERRIES AND LATER OF STEWED PRUNES AND LEATHER.
THEY ARE A PERFECT MATCH FOR A MAGRET OR CONFIT DE CANARD.

most sought-after *terroirs* are those that produce the white wines that are among the most elegant in the whole of France. They include Clos Lapeyre, Clos Thou, and Domaine de Larredya. As a sublime accompaniment to both sweet and savory dishes, foie gras, and fruity desserts, a Jurançon dessert wine can rival the finest Sauternes. Madiran, a wine that for a long time was used purely for celebrating Mass, enjoyed fame beyond the French borders thanks to the pilgrims making their arduous way through Southwest France to the shrine of Santiago de Compostela. Made in Gascony in the same region as Pacherenc de Vic-Bilh, Madiran is a powerful red that needs long maturing, the perfect accompaniment to foie gras, a fruit-based dessert, or a platter of local cheeses such as Ossau Iraty or Tomme.

Downstream of Madiran, the Tursan VDQS is currently on the rise. The appellation produces mostly reds, but the fragrant, dry, lively whites are more interesting. These appellations are part of the Pyrenean vineyard, one of whose greatest advocates is Michel Guérard, famous chef and owner of Les Prés d'Eugénie at Eugénie-les-Bains, which has earned the coveted three Michelin stars. Tursan is a wine of smooth tannins that enlivens the dishes of this district famous for its fine food.

In the Cahors region, alongside the stands of corn and sunflowers, the vines are cultivated in an English-style setting with lawns, rose bushes, and hedges. Just north of Toulouse, the Côtes du Frontonnais offers simple and fruity reds and rosés, such as those of Château de Bellevue-la-Forêt, Château Le Roc, and Domaine de Joliet. Along with Gaillac, these three appellations come from the Pyrenean highlands.

Further downstream lies the VDQS Côtes-du-Brulhois, which produces lighter wines. The red is the perfect accompaniment to white meats, while the rosé should be drunk young, with cured meats or broiled meats and salads. Buzet lies on the left bank of the Garonne, north of the vines grown for the production of Armagnac, and encompasses twenty-seven *communes*, grouped around a cooperative that offers high-quality wines. The top wine, the Cuvée Napoléon, has something in common with the great man in that it is small—but very big! Heading north are the Côtes du Marmandais with its unusual Abouriou vine, an early-ripening, resistant variety. This small detour has brought us to the edge of Aquitaine.

As can be seen, there is no uniformity here. The vine prospers in scattered regions, each of which has a strong tradition linked to local varieties. In some appellations reds, whites, and rosés are made, while others are devoted entirely to white or red. For the newcomer, it can be a confusing situation. But the good news for wine lovers is that the great and generous Southwest offers a vast range of diverse and original wines all the more likeable for being moderately priced.

THE VINES OF JURANÇON, THE BAPTISMAL WINE OF HENRI IV, CARPET THE FOOTHILLS OF THE MAJESTIC PYRENEES AND YIELD SUBTLE DESSERT WINES AND AROMATIC DRY WHITES.

CAHORS:
BETWEEN PLATEAU AND RIVER

The wines of Cahors are underrated, little known, and suffer from an outdated and unfair image as the favorite tipple of the French blue-collar worker. They certainly have body and structure, but they are not heavy. Robust but never crude, they are supple and rich in tannins, with a dense, velvety texture. Although their register of aromas is extensive, the most frequent notes are those of cherry, raspberry, red currant, and black currant. A delicious range! They evolve in the mouth with notes of vanilla and licorice, eventually merging into a well-balanced whole. Although Cahors wine used to have the reputation of being drinkable only if aged, the development of modern grape-growing and winemaking methods makes it possible to enjoy these wines young. Of all the wines of Southwest France, these are the ones that can claim to have improved the most spectacularly, and the most enthusiastic advocates of these improvements are the people who live in the *département* of Lot-et-Garonne.

The vineyard extends westward in the direction of Luzech, covering 10,500 acres (4,250 hectares). It hugs the banks of the river, covering the terraced slopes or spreading over the limestone plateau known as a *causse*. The first winemakers here were strongly influenced by Roman vinification methods, but showed their ingenuity by making a few improvements, notably the invention of the wooden barrel. This made it possible to replace the traditional terracotta amphora for storage, making it easier to preserve the wine and transport it over water. The barrels were sent down the river Lot on the flat-bottomed barges known as *gabarres*, which remained in use until the early twentieth century.

Situated between the forty-fourth and forty-fifth parallels, the Cahors region is equidistant as the crow flies from the Atlantic, the Mediterranean, and the Pyrenees. This position protects it from both Atlantic humidity and the autumn rains of the northern Mediterranean and blesses it with Indian summers that favor the full ripening of the grapes by harvest time. The grape-growing area covers two very different types of terrain. The first is the valley of the river Lot; the other, set slightly back from the river, covers the *causse*. Beside the Lot, the limestone bedrock is covered by a rich layer of alluvial soil leeched from the river and its tributaries, and containing pebbles, gravel, and stones dislodged through erosion. The soil of the limestone plateau is shallower, consisting of clay-covered rocks mixed with marl. So does this mean that the vines grown on terraces are well structured and those grown on the plateau are more aromatic? No, because the local winemakers are skilled enough to extract the best from this alliance between the limestone soil and the alluvial accretions.

The main variety, Malbec or Côt, is known here as Auxerrois and represents 70 percent of total plantings. This variety gives Cahors wine its characteristic color and ability to age, as well as the tannin-rich temperament that delights lovers of strong wines. The second most popular variety is Merlot, originally from the Bordeaux region. It makes the wine fuller, mellower, and more aromatic. Tannat, from Madiran, reinforces the qualities of the principal varieties, resulting in a wine that can age in the bottle.

Cahors is considered to be both one of the oldest and one of the newest vineyards of France. Although it was originally planted by the Romans more than two thousand years ago, it was first decimated by the phylloxera plague in the late nineteenth century and destroyed for a second time by the devastating frost of 1956. Vines were replanted immediately, but it was not until the 1970s that the wine reappeared in large quantities in Paris, thanks to its most loyal advocate, President Georges Pompidou, who swore by Clos de Gamot, owned by the Jouffreau family, a dynasty of winemakers since 1610.

THE UNDERGROUND CELLARS OF THE CHÂTEAU DE MERCUÈS HOLD NEARLY FOUR HUNDRED
CASKS IN WHICH THE ESTATE'S RED IS AGED FOR TWELVE MONTHS BEFORE BEING BOTTLED.
THE RESULTING WINE IS CONCENTRATED, WITH VELVETY TANNINS AND A FRAGRANCE
OF DARK BERRIES, PROVING THAT POWER AND ELEGANCE CAN COEXIST IN CAHORS.

Famous personalities such as the queen of Denmark and successful French businessman Alain-Dominique Perrin have fallen under the spell of the Lot and its wines, acquiring châteaux in the region and helping to make the appellation famous throughout the world. Since 1971, the date on which the wine acquired Appellation d'Origine Contrôlée status, everything has been done to transform the "black wine" into a product of quality, made by 478 producers, either grouped into cooperatives or operating as independent growers and winemakers.

ITINERARY

Like Bordeaux and Gaillac, the town of Cahors has lent its name to the wine. The first rows of vines can be seen starting from the village of Mercuès, which lies about five miles north of the seat of the *département*, on the right bank of the river. The village is dominated by a castle, the Castrum Mercurii, from which it takes its name. The historical value of the magnificent Château de Mercuès, an imposing pile built to a vertiginous height, is equaled by that of its wines. The vineyard extends over one hundred acres (forty hectares) and has been replanted at a relatively high density of 2,700 plants per acre (6,700 per hectare), compared with an average density of 1,620 per acre (4,000 per hectare) for the region, resulting in improved quality and yields. Vinification at the château takes place parcel by parcel to extract the best from the land. The grapes thus obtained are richer, producing wines that are concentrated and elegant. This is illustrated particularly well by the 1995 vintage, the best of the last decade.

The restaurant at Château de Mercuès provides a feast of the most delicious local fare, a real gourmet treat and testament to the bounty of nature. The farmland bordering the Lot produces the finest produce. Truffles, foie gras, saffron, poultry, lamb, walnuts, melons, Cabécou goat cheese, and cheeses bearing the Rocamadour appellation offer a feast of flavors, gracing the tables of homes and restaurants in the region and well beyond. They are the perfect accompaniment to the local wines.

Downstream of Mercuès is Caillac, home to the Château de Laroque, perched high on the hilltop as if standing guard over the river below, and the Château de Lagrézette, owned by Alain-Dominique Perrin, former president and CEO of the luxury goods firm Cartier.

Lagrézette was built in the fifteenth century, a combination of monumental architecture in the medieval tradition and fine Renaissance ornamentation. Alain-Dominique Perrin bought it in 1980 in a return to his original vocation, that of winemaking. The château became a listed historic monument in 1982. The house itself is not open to the public, but the cellar is well worth visiting. You enter through a handsome carved wooden door, but before being tempted by a few bottles, take the time to admire the *chai*. Unique of its type, it has been built on three levels underground and is 148 feet (forty-five meters) long and sixty-two feet (nineteen meters) wide. Its layout is dictated by a desire for maximum efficiency. The grapes are picked by hand and sorted manually, then destemmed and pressed on level three. Fermentation takes place on level two in temperature-controlled stainless steel vats with a reduced capacity, enabling plot-by-plot vinification. The must is aged in barrels on level one, where the temperature and humidity are naturally ideal and constant. The grapes are moved from one level to another by force of gravity. In short, it is well worth a look even before you take a drink. During your visit to Château de Lagrézette, look out for the famous dovecote among

THE CHÂTEAU DE CAÏX (FAR LEFT), LOCATED IN LUZECH, IS THE FRENCH RESIDENCE OF THE DANISH ROYAL FAMILY. THE WINES MADE HERE, SUCH AS THE CIGARELLE, ARE FULL AND RICH. WITH ITS HANDSOME DARK APPEARANCE, THE CLOS DE GAMOT (LEFT), WHOSE GREATEST ADVOCATE WAS THE FRENCH PRESIDENT GEORGES POMPIDOU, GIVES OF ITS BEST AFTER BEING AGED FOR MANY YEARS IN THE BARREL. THE CHÂTEAU DE MERCUÈS (FACING PAGE), A LUXURY HOTEL AND RESTAURANT COMBINED WITH A WINEMAKING ESTATE, OFFERS THE FINEST CUISINE IN THE REGION.

the first rows of vines; this was the inspiration for the name of the estate's best wine.

From Château de Lagrézette, Saint-Vincent-Rive-d'Olt can be reached by following the D8. This little town bears the old name of the river (Olt/Lot) and is under the protection of Saint Vincent, patron saint of winemakers. The village adjoins the Lot on the western side, which ensures that the climate is temperate and that the limestone soil has the lightness so favorable to grape-growing. The hamlet of Marcayrac lies on the left bank of the stream, clinging to the north-facing slope of a hill that is 1,280 feet (390 meters) high. The vine occupies a central place throughout the district. Until recently, the winemakers here brought their harvest to the cooperative cellar, but today the younger generation is tending to make its own wines.

Although the distance from Saint-Vincent-Rive-d'Olt to Puy-l'Évêque is just over ten miles as the crow flies, the winding Lot covers three times as many miles. Thanks to this meandering course and the undulating topography, the vines are able to benefit from a special microclimate.

The Château de Caïx, on the right bank of the river, clinging to a flank of the *causse* upstream of Luzech, is a magnificent seventeenth-century property, flanked by two round towers that are reflected in the water. In the eighteenth century, the Marquis Lefranc de Pompignan, a member of the Académie Française and a sworn enemy of Voltaire, converted this feudal bastion into a pleasant residence. The vineyard, nestling in a meander of the Lot, has a southern exposure, thus benefiting from an ideal amount of sunshine. It spreads over limestone terraces dug into the hillside right down to the gravel of the riverside. Downstream of the property, the *chai* blends well with the landscape and architecture of the château. The Château de Caïx is, in fact, famous well beyond the borders of France, thanks to its royal owner. Since 1975, it has been the summer residence of the queen of Denmark. Her husband, Prince Henri de Monpezat, is a native of this region and he

bought, restored, and then replanted the vineyard. Every year thousands of Danes make the pilgrimage to the royal wine cellar in order to buy a few sovereign bottles, including the very successful Marches de Caïx and La Cigaralle.

Every May, in the cellars of the village of Albas, an ancient Roman fortress that was the residence of the bishops of Cahors in the Middle Ages, more than four thousand people come to raise their glasses and sing the praises of Auxerrois, the local grape variety. During this night of music and wine, groups of musicians improvise miniature concerts in the cellars, while the winemakers throw themselves into hearty drinking songs—until they are no longer thirsty. During the celebration, the steep street (the only street in the village, in fact) is transformed by lively festivities worthy of a Spanish *feria*.

When leaving Albas and its episcopal château for the D37 in the direction of Sauzet, it is worth stopping to admire the view over the vine-covered valley. After a large bend in the river, a halt at Bélaye, and a few more rows of vines, you will arrive at Puy-l'Évêque. It is easy to imagine the time when the town was a famous port on the wine route, and you can still see the quay where the *gabarres*, the wine barges, moored. From here right to the edge of the *département*, whichever direction you go in, all the roads are lined with rows of vines. Around Puy-l'Évêque, the very heart of the vineyard, you can visit some of the most famous estates of the appellation, such as the Château du Cayrou. In 1971, the Jouffreau family, winemakers from father to son for seven centuries, bought this magnificent château. Although it dates back even further, the current elegant pale stone and pink brick façade, with its mullioned windows and sculpture of the Virgin Mary standing in an alcove over the front door, was built between the fourteenth and sixteenth centuries. Cayrou has magnificent grounds, home to more than sixty different species of tree, including cedars that are several hundred years old. In the attractive wine-tasting cellar that is also used for exhibitions of paintings, you can sample several wines from Château du Cayrou, as well as those made at Clos de Gamot, which is owned by two sisters in this same family. The various *cuvées* on offer are fine, aristocratic, elegant wines—classics of the appellation.

Château Lamartine is situated at the western edge of the appellation, where the valley opens out into the wide plains of the Lot-et-Garonne famous for their orchards. It has seventy-four acres (thirty hectares) under cultivation, the vines facing directly southeast, encouraging early ripening. Here, the soil is worked in traditional ways, but using modern tools. The harvest is sorted by hand and only the best grapes are used, with about one third being

THE BULGING FAÇADES OF THE CHÂTEAU DE LA GRÉZETTE
SEEM TO ENHANCE THE FLOWING LINES OF THE FAMOUS
SEVENTEENTH-CENTURY DOVECOTE THAT HAS LENT ITS NAME
TO THE ESTATE'S BEST CUVÉE. THE WINE IS AGED FOR TWENTY-
EIGHT MONTHS IN OAK BARRELS AND ITS FINESSE, POWER, AND
CONCENTRATION RIVAL THOSE OF A BORDEAUX GRAND CRU.

rejected. Maceration is prolonged, lasting up to forty days depending on the vintage. Although their standard red is very pleasant, the Cuvée Particulière is made from the oldest vines on the property and has a combination of harmony, elegance, and power. The top wine is the Cuvée Expression, which is aged for twenty months in new barrels from a very low yield—one bottle being the equivalent of the yield from one vine plant. Seeking maximum concentration rather than maximum extraction, the wines of Alain Gayraud are the finest expression of the Auxerrois variety.

Not far from Château Lamartine, the Domaine du Cèdre at Vire-sur-Lot sets the standard by which all Cahors wines should be judged. Although there is nothing exceptional about the building, the wines that can be bought here are remarkable. The vines cover an area of sixty acres (twenty-five hectares) and are grown without the aid of chemicals. Skill, meticulousness, and talent are the three virtues of Pascal and Jean-Marc Verhaeghe-Bru, who work their vines with the care of goldsmiths. They favor low yields, harvesting the grapes when they are at their peak of ripeness, and use malolactic fermentation in wooden vats. The resulting wines are very dark in color and are characterized by their harmony, finesse, roundness, and concentration. The Prestige and Le Cèdre *cuvées* are exceptional, but all of the estate's wines are well made.

According to tradition, the peasants harvested at night in order to be able to keep some of the harvest for themselves, instead of delivering it all to the lord of the manor as they were supposed to. Jean-Luc Baldès of Clos Triguedina also picks his grapes by moonlight, but that is because harvesting in the cool of the evening is said to preserve the aromas. With its elegantly woody notes, this winemaker's Prince Probus has been one of the appellation's great, and most mysterious, wines for more than twenty years. If you only get the chance to taste one Cahors wine, it ought to be this one, because Maître Baldès is, by common consent, one of the most talented winemakers in the region. With his customary curiosity and openmindedness, he has also attempted to produce a white based on Chardonnay and Viognier, with considerable success. The result is a supple wine with great finesse that can be drunk as an aperitif or as a wonderful accompaniment to cheeses such as Comté. All this goes to show that in Cahors nothing is impossible.

NAMED AFTER A LANDMARK ON THE ESTATE, DOMAINE COSSE MAISONNEUVE'S LES LAQUETS (BELOW) IS A SUBTLE WINE WITH A NOSE OF BLACK CURRANT, MULBERRY, AND SPICES AND A POTENTIAL AS GREAT AS THAT OF LE CÈDRE, THE TOP WINE FROM THE SAME DOMAINE, WHICH HAS AN AROMA OF RUSSIAN LEATHER. THE OLD CASKS IN THE CELLAR AT CHÂTEAU DU CAYROU CONTAIN DARK, STRONG RED WINES (FACING PAGE).

GAILLAC:
THREE TERROIRS, ONE APPELLATION

—————

When you are in the Tarn you are already in the Midi. But this is a Midi with an Occitan accent, full of greenery, old-fashioned courtesy, brick-built houses, and welcoming faces. A Midi of roads shaded with plane trees, peaceful but far from monotonous valleys, medieval villages, mischievous rivers, renovated country homes, and serried rows of grapevines. A Midi bursting with talent, yet disconcerting in its modesty. A Midi that is eco-friendly, natural, and well preserved. In short, this is an old-fashioned Midi, simple and charming.

The *département* of Tarn was once part of the province of Languedoc and today it is proud to be part of the greater Midi-Pyrénées region. It is scarcely forty-five miles from the Rouergue, the famous Gorges du Tarn, the Cévennes, and the sea. In other words, the Tarn vineyards are the most Mediterranean in type of the Midi-Pyrénées region. The Gaillac appellation surrounds the town of the same name, and stretches along both banks of the river Tarn, reaching as far as the medieval city of Cordes-sur-Ciel. Grape-growing in the region started in antiquity, but it was the Benedictine monks of the abbey of Saint-Michel de Gaillac who started it in earnest. The wines were sent down the Tarn on barges toward the Garonne and this nectar went on to conquer France and the neighboring countries. François I, Henri III, and Louis XIV made no secret of their passion for this spiritual beverage. In the seventeenth century, the Vins du Coq, named for the rooster branded on the barrels, had such a good reputation that they were exported to England, Flanders, the Netherlands, Russia, and Scandinavia. The vineyards suffered a reversal of fortune, however, when Bordeaux banned the sale of wines from these eastern highlands until its own stocks were exhausted.

It was not until 1938 that the white wines of the region were awarded Appellation d'Origine Contrôlée status, and not until 1970 that the red wines received that distinction. Today, the vineyards cover about 9,500 acres (3,850 hectares) and produce twenty-two million bottles a year, thanks to the expertise of 410 winemakers. Clearly, Gaillac is more than a mere wine, for its prosperity has enabled it to become one of the great ambassadors of Southwest France.

Gaillac has three distinct areas, a temperate microclimate, and its own specific grape varieties, all of which enable it to produce an incredible range of wines, rivaled by few other French regions. There are dry whites, sweet whites, slightly sparkling wines, sparkling wines, reds, and young (*primeur*) wines.

The terraced plantings on the left bank of the Tarn extend for about twenty miles between Florentin and Couffouleux, via sun-drenched Técou and Peyrole. The red wines from this area are full-bodied and have a deep garnet color. The aromas are rich and luxuriant, a combination of jams, black currant, and spices. They are full of character and age well.

The local Loin de l'Oeil variety endows the whites with an aroma of fragrant blossoms and peaches. The *terroir* here is ideal for producing superb white dessert wines that are complex and flavorsome. Across the river, grapes grown on the slopes of the right bank produce different wines, in a vast vineyard stretching from Castelnau-de-Lévis, past Lisle-sur-Tarn, to Rabastens. They benefit from a full southern exposure and are protected by the forests of Grésigne and Sivens. Conditions here are ideal for the red Duras and Syrah varieties, whose spicy flavors mingle harmoniously with the wilder fragrances of Braucol. Further north, on the Cestayrols plateau, the dry whites and slightly sparkling wines have crisp, floral notes and a light, fruity flavor.

The rolling hills of the Gaillac appellation receive the full force of the hot, dry southerly winds that blow in from the Mediterranean.

THE MAISON DE LA VIGNE ET DU VIN, HOUSED IN THE TWELFTH-CENTURY ABBEY
OF SAINT-MICHEL ON THE BANKS OF THE RIVER TARN, IS A SHOWCASE FOR GAILLAC WINES.
ALL THE TOP WINES OF THE APPELLATION CAN BE FOUND HERE.

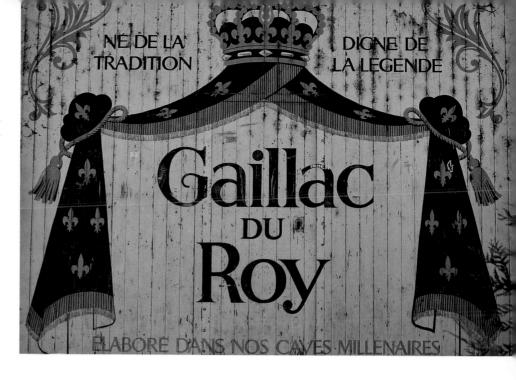

BETWEEN CORDES AND CASTELNAU-DE-MONTMIRAIL,
A HOUSE THAT IS TYPICAL OF THE TARN DÉPARTEMENT,
STANDING AMONG THE VINES OF THE CORDES PLATEAU.

Thanks in part to this climate, the white wines are subtle, elegant, and long on the palate, while the reds are robust, full-bodied, fruity, with well-rounded tannins. The red wines produced from grapes grown on the slopes of Lisle-sur-Tarn and Rabastens are powerful and warm, with blended tannins, while the whites are distinguished by their delicate fragrance. On the Cordais plateau, which is located in the northern part of the Gaillac region, the harvest is later, giving the wines greater finesse, aroma, and fruit flavors. This combination of climatic and geological conditions results in distinguished and elegant wines: the whites are crisp, fruity, and rich in floral aromas, while the reds are well balanced, full of personality, and very drinkable. They are ready for drinking after one year, but can be laid down for up to six years. The rosés are fragrant, light, and bursting with fruit, making them wonderfully thirst-quenching. They are made exclusively from Gamay, vinified using unpressed whole grapes, and cannot be drunk until the third Thursday in November. Needless to say, that Thursday is always festive.

What makes this vine-growing area even more original is the fact that, just east of Albi, it contains a small, underrated plot of land known as the Noyau de Cunac.

If you ask Robert Plageoles, the owner of Très Cantous, he will affirm that more than twenty different varieties are used in making Gaillac. This great expert can list seven varieties of Mauzac, and he also owns some very old varieties, such as Verdanel and Ombenc. Although over the centuries, some varieties have disappeared completely, to be replaced by new ones, the Gaillac appellation still permits five varieties to be used for making white wines, and six for reds. Mauzac is a traditional variety of this region, found only in Limoux, and it is used to great effect in the production of all the white wines, dry, sweet, and sparkling. The grape has a rich fragrance of apple and pear, and provides a hint of acidity. As a varietal wine, pure Mauzac is a marvel.

Loin-de-l'Oeil, from the Provençal *len-de-l'el* ("far from the eye"), was so called because the grape bunches have a very long stalk and the grape is far from the *oeil* (eye), or bud that gave birth to it. This very old variety is only found in Gaillac. It produces a crisp, smooth wine with subtle, floral aromas, and it combines very well with Mauzac.

Duras is one of the region's oldest varieties and was reintroduced twenty years ago. It lends color, body, and finesse to a wine. Its main characteristics are its pear and spice aromas. It does not age well and is therefore ideal for the Gaillac rosé. Braucol, also known as Fer-Servadou, is a hardy grape that gives wines color and strength. Its distinctive aromas have a hint of black currant, strawberry, bruised leaves, and bell pepper. Sauvignon, Muscadelle, Ondenc, and Sémillon are used to supplement the traditional Gaillac varieties.

The white wines of Gaillac are said to be the most popular Midi-Pyrénées wines with women. They are fresh and subtle, and are made as both dry and dessert wines. The dry white is a blend of local grape varieties, and can be identified by its straw color, subtly shot with shades of green. It is intensely fruity and delicately structured, with entrancing aromas. It should be drunk very cold. The famous Gaillac Perlé is a semi-sparkling white wine that has kept its natural fizz. It is light, fruity, and fresh, tickling the tongue enticingly. An ideal aperitif wine or accompaniment to seafood, it should be drunk well chilled.

The famous Gaillac dessert wine, made from the oldest vines, has glorious aromas of Bartlett pears, toffee apple, honey, and figs, and is smooth and long in the mouth. It can be served as an aperitif or with dessert, and is a good choice to accompany foie gras and Roquefort cheese. It is important to note that it must be drunk before its tenth birthday. It is one of the best French sparkling wines, and is available *brut* (bone dry), *demi-sec* (medium dry), and *doux* (sweet). It is best drunk between 44°F and 46°F (7°C to 8°C). The *brut* is perfect as an aperitif, while the *doux* is naturally to be drunk with or after dessert.

ITINERARY

Gaillac, situated in the northwest of the *département*, has existed as a separate district since 952, thanks to its position in a loop of the river Tarn. It is an attractive jumble of arcaded squares, steep, narrow streets, half-timbered houses, and elegant town houses. Wine and blue dye from woad were responsible for the town's prosperity and renown, and you are constantly reminded of this. If you walk down the pedestrianized rue Portal, it is worth making a detour to the Petite Cave on rue Joseph-Rigal to let yourself be tempted by some rare wines. For forty-one years, Madame Motte has been offering vintages that are otherwise impossible to find. There is nothing about the Gaillac vineyards that this cheerful lady does not know, and she has over five hundred wines to refer to. The brick-built, seventeenth-century Château de Foucaud houses a museum of fine art. For twenty-five years, it has also hosted the famous Fête des Vins de Gaillac, held in August. This festival offers a rare opportunity to meet vine growers and winemakers, with plenty of fun tastings, events, and an evening of dancing and fireworks. It is one of the biggest events on the calendar for the town's inhabitants. The abbey of Saint-Michel houses the Maison de la Vigne et du Vin, and is a good stopping-off point on the tour. It is used as a showcase for Gaillac wines and has a wine-tasting room where you can purchase some excellent bottles.

Another place that should not be missed is the home of Robert Plageoles, Domaine des Très Cantous. Like it or not, it is to the talent of this French winemaker and media star that the Gaillac appellation largely owes its fame. His status can be gauged from the fact that 65 percent of Michelin-starred restaurants buy their wine from him. "A winemaker aware of his environment," as he likes to describe himself, he works alongside the INRA (French national institute for agricultural research) and the CNRS (French center for scientific research). In fact, his estate produces only small quantities of rare and expensive wine. Here, in his museum-cum-home, you will learn that, within the whole appellation, only about twelve acres (five hectares) are planted with Ombenc, that Mauzac has been cultivated as far back as the Gallic era, that the Duras vine comes from Italy, and that, just before the big freeze of 1956, the vineyards covered about 96,000 acres (39,000 hectares), whereas they now cover less than 22,000 acres (9,000 hectares).

When you leave Domaine des Très Cantous, just continue beside the vines and follow the road that winds through the dry and dusty fields to the Château de Salettes. Here, wealth is flaunted. The walls have been rebuilt, the roof repaired, and the cobblestones

THE VINEYARDS OF GAILLAC ARE THOUGHT TO BE THE OLDEST
IN THE SOUTHWEST. A WIDE VARIETY OF GRAPES IS GROWN
HERE AND THE APPELLATION COVERS EVERY TYPE OF WINE,
FROM SWEET DESSERT WINES TO SPARKLING WINES AND EVEN
A RED PRIMEUR.

CHÂTEAU DE SAURS ON THE RIGHT BANK OF THE TARN IS
ONE OF THE MOST IMPRESSIVE IN THE GAILLAC REGION.
IN THE HANDSOME BRICK CELLARS, BOTH DRY AND SWEET
WHITES ARE MADE, TOGETHER WITH RICH, FORTHRIGHT REDS.

scoured. The owner, the French mastermind behind nuclear imaging, has painstakingly restored the château to its former glory. From the outer walls to the spiral staircases, every last detail has been thought of. It is the perfect place to stay for a couple of days. In this restful château, which also produces wines, you can attend specialist tastings and, of course, purchase wine that is always highly rated in the guides.

From Campagnac you can appreciate the endless view over the Grésigne forest, which is regarded as one of the most beautiful oak groves in southern France. The road around this small, vine-encircled village has many wonderful vantage points at each bend. From here, the vineyard can be seen at its best, laid out in carefully arranged rows, with an almost military precision. The road takes you all the way to the Château de Mayragues, which has a listed, seventeenth-century dovecote. This residence received the Grand Prix des Vieilles Maisons Françaises in 1998 and is one of the three most beautiful winemaking properties in the Tarn, along with the Château de Saurs and the Château de Lastours. Owner Alan Geddes is a Scot married to a Parisian and his passion for wine has led him to cultivate his single forty-four-acre (eighteen-hectare) spread using biodynamic methods. Wines are made using the most traditional methods. Yields are small and the resulting wines are exceptional. The Blanc Doux is syrupy in texture, with citrus aromas that are not overpowered by sweetness. The château is a delight for lovers of ancient stonework and decoration, and has two guest rooms.

Take the RN88 to return to Gaillac. At about the halfway point, a majestic avenue lined with three-hundred-year-old plane trees leads to Château Lastours. This elegant seventeenth-century residence of flint and brick reclines lazily on a huge terrace that follows the curve of the river. There are magnificent gardens with panoramic views and the excellent wines regularly receive awards. They include the dry white Les Graviers and the Cuvée Spéciale, a low-yield wine made from old Sémillon and Sauvignon vines. This is enough to make Lastours an unforgettable stop, and the owners, the Faramoud family, recommend an exciting tour, both historic and viticultural, which includes a visit to the *chais*.

Rabastens is the favorite vacation destination for the citizens of Toulouse. The little town extends along several bends of the river. It is impossible to visit it without dropping in on the cooperative, created in 1953 by a group of vine growers who wanted to pool their experience and resources. Today it encompasses about 3,200 acres (1,290 hectares) of vineyard and 240 growers. These growers have now inherited the vineyard of the counts of Toulouse, and they respect a tradition of craftsmanship in grape-growing and wine-making. Make sure you leave plenty of time for tasting the wine.

MADIRAN AND PACHERENC DU VIC-BILH:
ONE VINEYARD, TWO APPELLATIONS

At the crossroads of the Bigorre, Béarn, and Armagnac regions there is a single *terroir* that has two Appellations d'Origine Contrôlées: Madiran for the reds and Pacherenc du Vic-Bilh for the whites. They bestride two cultures, those of Gascony and Béarn, and two administrative regions, Aquitaine and the Midi-Pyrénées, as well as three *départements* (Pyrénées-Atlantiques, Hautes-Pyrénées, and Gers) and four valleys. The Madiran appellation leapfrogs its way between thirty-six *communes*. Its strong, tannic wine needs bottle aging. After two or three years, it develops fragrances of berries and spices, the tannins become softer and more refined, and a wide range of flavors emerge—spices, cocoa, vanilla, a hint of roasted coffee. It should be served at a temperature of 57°F to 59°F (16°C to 18°C) and makes a wonderful companion to local dishes such as steak with *sauce béarnaise*, *confits*, duck breast, roast lamb, and Pyrenean cheeses. It also goes very well with salami, game, and red meats—but only on condition that it is not drunk too young.

The only French wine that is required to age for at least one year, Madiran is claimed to have curative properties. It is very rich in polyphenols, and has the highest anthocyanin content of any French wine, and thus of resveratrol, which is supposed to be beneficial to the cardiovascular system. Consequently, Madiran could be seen as being a wine of the heart.

The little vineyard known as Pacherenc du Vic-Bilh covers 370 acres (150 hectares). Its name means "old country" in Gascon, and it covers the same geographical area as the Madiran appellation. The wine won appellation status in 1975, and has a rich aromatic palette thanks to the varieties from which it is made, namely Courbu, Arruffiat (or Ruffiac), Camaralet, and Manseng, together with Sauvignon and Sémillon. The wine is generally dry and may be smooth or lively, but must have a minimum alcohol content of 12 percent. The honeyed flavor is reminiscent of that of its big brother, Jurançon, with delicate nuances of flowers and tropical fruits. It is harvested late (sometimes as late as New Year's Eve!), so that the sugar-saturated grapes give it a slightly syrupy quality. When dry, it should be drunk chilled at 46°F (8°C) within three or four years of harvesting. It goes particularly well with shellfish and fish baked in sauce. As for the dessert variety, it is unctuous and powerful, with a fruity, honeyed flavor. It can be drunk as an aperitif or as an accompaniment to foie gras or sheep's milk cheese.

The 5,000 acres (2,000 hectares) of vines are shared between the two appellations and the VDQS Côtes de Saint-Mont. Madiran is made in an area of around 2,700 acres (1,100 hectares), where the soil is a mixture of limestone and clay that is well suited to red grape varieties. The dry whites and dessert wines of Pacherenc come from areas where the soil consists mainly of clay and silica. The slopes are separated by deep valleys, becoming less high toward the north, and culminating in narrow outcrops of rock above the Adour valley. These hills, into which narrow perpendicular gorges have been cut over the centuries, have south-facing slopes that are particularly suitable for growing vines. The Madiran-producing district can be divided in three distinct areas: Pacherenc du Vic-Bilh country, consisting of steep hills or west-facing slopes; the most characteristic area of the Madiran appellation on the eastern slopes, which produces intense, black, concentrated wines; and finally the remaining area of hills, covered in clay soil filled with pebbles that favor the production of intense, rounded wines with full tannins.

In this very southerly vineyard (Pau lies further south than Nice), the old vine stocks continue to be grown, and some of these plots that were spared the ravages of phylloxera contain vines that are more than a hundred years old. Also, it is not unusual to find wild vines, known as *lambrusques*, growing along hedges and mountain streams.

MADIRAN IS FAMOUS FOR ITS AGING POTENTIAL AND SHOULD BE LEFT IN THE CELLAR
FOR A GOOD TEN YEARS TO MATURE WHILE THE ASTRINGENT TANNINS GRADUALLY SOFTEN.

RED VARIETIES

Tannat: Like the inhabitants of the Béarn region, it is pretty temperamental. This hardy plant does not fear heavy rain or drought, but it is difficult to tame, often tough and aggressive, sometimes green and astringent. On the other hand, the grapes are very juicy and produce a wine, rich in color and tannins, that requires a lot of expertise and patience on the part of the winemaker. Tannat is the appellation's principal variety, and it is only grown in the Val d'Adour, where favorable fall conditions enable it to reach complete ripeness. When the wine is young, the aromas of soft fruits and berries (black currant, mulberry, gooseberry) contrast with the surprisingly full tannins. With aging, these tannins develop roundness and finesse, with fragrances ranging from spices, roasted coffee, and cocoa to vanilla.

Cabernet Franc: This variety comes from the Bordeaux region and provides marked fragrance and a certain mellowness. Fruity, supple, rounded, harmonious, and easy to control, it is the ideal partner for Tannat.

Fer-Servadou or Pinenc: With its rounded structure, culminating in rich, fine tannins, this variety is very aromatic, introducing balsamic fragrances of ivy, mint, and orange peel. As it ages, it develops pleasantly pronounced black currant notes.

WHITE VARIETIES

Arrufiac: Although, in normal circumstance, this variety is reserved for dry Pacherenc, it can also be used in the final blend of sweet wines for the finest vintages. Its floral and balsamic aromas, with a certain flinty note, encapsulate the essence of Pacherenc.

Petit Courbu: Whether vinified as a dry or sweet wine, its fragrances have a certain floral exoticism. Its structure in the mouth, allied to great length and fullness, provide the foundations for good sweet wine.

Gros Manseng: This variety is often reserved for dry Pacherencs, and has a strong nose of pineapple and grapefruit combined with acacia flower and spice notes.

The Romans, who appreciated the richness and sensuous pleasures of this region, introduced the grape vine in the second century A.D., as can be seen from the mosaics uncovered during archeological digs at Taron. The wine was used for celebrating Mass throughout the diocese, later becoming famous through the pilgrims on their way to the shrine of Santiago de Compostela, who would stop over at the abbey of Madiran, founded in 1030. When the Béarn region was occupied by the Black Prince, who became Prince of Aquitaine in 1360, the English discovered this powerful wine, with its excellent keeping qualities. It was thus exported in large quantities to England, where Edward II, father of the Black Prince, adopted it as a wine for special occasions. Soon, the whole of northern Europe came to value it, and François I described it as "the wine of the aristocracy, powerful, high in

flavor and crimson in color." While the local customers, the peasants and shepherds of the Pyrenees, wanted "black" wines that were coarse and thick, the urbanization of Europe in the eighteenth and nineteenth centuries created wine drinkers who preferred more refined products. For instance, from the eighteenth century onward, the Dutch market showed a preference for "sweet" white wines and those made from the "piquepout" (picpoul) variety used for distilling into brandy. Wines were so important to the region that in 1818, in the *commune* of Madiran alone, 909 acres (368 hectares) were under vine cultivation.

The approved growing area was sketched out in 1910, becoming the appellation Madiran et Pacherenc du Vic-Bilh in 1948, the creation of which helped producers to weather the postwar depression. In 1981, vine-growers on the right bank of the river Adour obtained a VDQS classification for Côtes de Saint-Mont. In their quest for quality, the local syndicates and cooperatives, such as the cooperative at Crouseilles and the Producteurs Plaimont, played a decisive role. They continue to guarantee the survival of small family wineries. By enabling them to concentrate on growing vines while entrusting the vinification and sale to others, they ensure that the highest winemaking standards are attained, something previously only within the means of the large estates that once dominated the Madiran district.

ITINERARY

The person who has put Madiran on the map in recent years is Alain Brumont, so our journey begins a few miles from Tarbes, at the home of this "working peasant" as he likes to call himself. Experimentation, innovation, and imagination are the watchwords of this iconoclastic, self-taught winemaker. He has two estates—the family property Château Bouscassé and Château Montus, which he bought in 1980—both dedicated to the glory of the Tannat variety. Relying on his instinct to begin with, he set out to produce a new kind of Madiran, seeking to enhance the fruit, suppleness, and balance. The result can be tasted in his Cuvée Prestige, which should be decanted three hours before drinking. This dark wine has an elegant nose of berries and undergrowth, with subtle musky notes. In the mouth it is oaky and fruity, with berry flavors and round tannins. Brumont replanted his vineyard, increasing the vine density, and each plot is harvested separately, with the grapes being pressed in separate vats. His extraordinary *chai* covers twenty thousand square feet (two thousand square meters) and houses nine oak vats used to make his finest wines. New wines have been developed, in which he is experimenting with new styles: Torus, which is intended to be drunk earlier; La Tyre, made from grapes from the highest plot in the appellation; and Les Menhirs, a combination of Tannat and Merlot. All of these wines are remarkable and can be found on the tables of the finest Michelin-starred restaurants, where they enhance the red-meat dishes and local specialties.

Not far from here, on a hilltop where the rows of vines face the Pyrenees, stands the Château d'Aydie, which has attractive, pointed turrets. Before this estate produced great wine, it was the home of French writer Joseph Peyré, winner of the prestigious Prix Goncourt literary prize, who was very attached to his region and his Béarnais manor house. The property was subsequently acquired by the Laplace family, which runs three estates and is famous for the high quality of its Tannat grapes. The Madiran and Pacherenc made by this family are among the finest produced, especially in the form of the Cuvée Prestige, the pride of the estate. It has an intense ruby red color, a subtle nose of berries and coffee, and a good attack in the

mouth, followed by great ripeness and silky tannins. The grapes are picked by hand and aged in new oak barrels for twelve to fourteen months. The wine is only bottled after it has been matured for twenty to twenty-four months, and has immense aging ability. After refurbishing the buildings and creating superb *chais*, this wine making dynasty radically rethought the vineyard. The number of vines was increased from four to eight thousand by adding a row of young vines in between two old ones. This was done with the aim of reducing the amount of grapes carried on each plant, while maintaining the yield, as in the major wine-producing regions. The Laplace family introduced stainless steel vats into the *chais*, as well as smaller wooden vats that are open to the skies. The aim was to improve the quality of the generic wines by increasing the percentage of Tannat. The result of this work was the Mansus Irani, named for a legionnaire who was stationed in the region. Here is perfect proof that Madiran can rival the great wines of Bordeaux.

If you take the route that leads from the D13 to the road through the valley of the Lées, you will see the Château d'Arricau-Bordes opposite. This beautifully restored château, surrounded by trees and flanked by its farm and *chais*, is currently run by the Crouseilles cooperative. The cooperative was created in the heart of the appellation in 1953 by a few enthusiastic vine growers. In 1981, it acquired the Château de Crouseilles, which soon became one of the best advertisements for the appellation and a symbol of Madiran. In 1999, the cooperative was voted *cave de l'année* by the *Revue des Vins de France*. One of the finest of its wines remains the Comte d'Orion, which will make you drunk—with pleasure!

The Château de Mascaraas is not far from the village of Garlin, the administrative center of the canton and starting point of the Madiran wine route. The estate makes a prestigious wine and has revitalized the western end of the appellation. With its magnificent view of the Pyrenees, this former hunting lodge of Jeanne d'Albret, queen of Navarre in the sixteenth century, is considered to be one of the finest châteaux in the Béarn. In an original move to meet the increasing demands of consumers, the contents of the wines can easily be monitored through an inscription on the capsule. This makes it possible to "trace" the wine from the bottle to the parcel of land, thanks to a computer program. With its ten acres (four hectares) planted with Madiran and two and a half acres (one hectare) planted with Pacherenc, Mascaraas is one of the treasures of the Crouseilles cooperative, as are the Château d'Arricau-Bordes and the Château de la Motte. Madiran goes from strength to strength.

IN THE BÉARN REGION, THE VINES CLOAK THE ROLLING HILLS, WHICH ARE DOTTED WITH WINEMAKING ESTATES LIKE DOMAINE CROUSEILLES (FACING PAGE). MADIRAN AND CÔTES DE SAINT-MONT (BELOW) ARE NEIGHBORING APPELLATIONS. THEIR DARK WINES, WITH THEIR RICH TANNINS THAT BECOME SILKY WITH AGE, ARE THE PERFECT ACCOMPANIMENT TO THE REGIONAL DISHES OF CONFIT DE CANARD AND GAME.

CÔTES DE SAINT-MONT:
BUDDING WINE

Gascony is a region of rich cuisine, conviviality, and characterful people. Its hilly landscape is also home to the little-known vineyard of Côtes de Saint-Mont, which became a VDQS in 1981. It is located in the west of the Gers, its slopes bounded by the river Adour and its tributaries, in a setting of steep valleys, meadows, woods, and fields of corn. The vines are cultivated over an area of 3,211 acres (1,300 hectares) and are an extension of the neighboring Madiran vineyard. Vines were first introduced here by the Greeks via Spain, and cultivation became extensive from 1050 onward following the foundation of the Saint-Mont monastery by Benedictine monks. The wines were famous from the eleventh century onward and were successfully exported until the nineteenth century, when phylloxera struck. After that, the region produced only one insignificant wine. In 1957, determined to prevent the ruination of such a fine *terroir*, a handful of winemakers decided to get together to create the Syndicat de Défense et de Promotion des Côtes de Saint-Mont. The first application for the title of Vin Délimité de Qualité Supérieure was rejected in 1975. With the help of the Institut National d'Appellations Contrôlées (INAO), the Syndicat reduced the growing area and abandoned the high yield policy in order to concentrate on quality, and in April 1981 VDQS status was granted. Quality has continued to improve steadily, suggesting that the Appellation d'Origine Contrôlée designation may not be far off.

Reds and rosés must contain at least 60 percent of the main grape variety, Tannat. Hand-picking is compulsory, and grapes must be picked off the bunch before being put into the vat, resulting in greater suppleness and less astringency. Juicy but refined, the wines have a different personality from those of neighboring Madiran. The reds from slopes exposed to the south and east are rounded and light. Those made from vines grown on gravelly soils should be drunk young. Heavy soils produce more powerful wines that are better suited for laying down, when the crimson of the young wine changes into a dark ruby in the bottle. The top wines, however, are garnet tinted with violet, turning to deep crimson with age.

The rosé wines must be made with at least 70 percent Tannat. They are lively and powerful, with a delicious nose of red berries, and in particular raspberry. In the mouth they are fresh, lively, and quite full.

The fine and elegant whites come from the steepest slopes exposed to the west and southwest. They are made from the Arrufiac variety, which is fresh, light, floral, and supple, from Petit Courbu, which is aromatic, floral, powerful, long, and round, as well as from more acidic varieties that provide power and liveliness, such as Petit Manseng and Gros Manseng, with their citrus fragrances. The young white wines are recognizable by their pale color and nose of soft fruits, such as peaches. As they age, the nose develops notes of tropical fruits. In the mouth, the wines are lively, fruity, and powerful, with a long finish.

Producteurs Plaimont manage 98 percent of the region's wines, encompassing 2,717 acres (1,100 hectares) of Saint-Mont, 555 acres (225 hectares) of Madiran, 111 acres (forty-five hectares) of Pacherenc, and 6,175 acres (2,500 hectares) of Vins de Pays des Côtes de Gascogne—which in all represents 1,350 winemakers. The name Plaimont is a contraction of the names of the three cooperatives: Plaisance, Aignan, and Saint-Mont. The federation was founded in 1979 under the impetus of André Dubosc, an agronomist specialized in viticulture and enology. Its watchwords are: "Rigor, strictness, dynamism." The Plaimont producers were pioneers in the technique of micro-oxygenation, a technique for controlling levels of oxygen during the winemaking process. Every aspect, from the selection of varieties to the management of plots, is computerized. In addition to supplying grapes for vinification, each

ALTHOUGH THE YOUNG CÔTES DE SAINT-MONT APPELLATION MOSTLY PRODUCES RED WINES,
ITS DRY WHITES ARE SUPPLE AND LIVELY AND ARE BEST SAVORED YOUNG, WHILE THEIR FRUITY FRAGRANCES ARE STILL STRONG.
THEY ARE PRESENTED IN THE MOST ATTRACTIVE BOTTLES.

Le Faîte
de Saint-Mont
2002

grower devotes one day per hectare and a half to the promotion of the wines, wearing his beret and apron. By creating vineyards around historic châteaux, the producers are not only contributing to the emergence of young winemakers, but they are also conducting a successful experiment in the preservation of the local heritage.

ITINERARY

This approach is exemplified by the Château de Sabazan, which is located in the medieval village of the same name and where life for the 150 inhabitants revolves around the vine. The village has a thirteenth-century Romanesque church and a château, which was rebuilt in the fifteenth century and is flanked by four large towers and a park. Sabazan also has a wonderful fountain—Perlette—designed more than four centuries ago and based on the one at the Villa Tivoli. The Producteurs Plaimont vinified the wines of this thirty-five acre (fourteen hectare) property for the first time in 1987. This was a pilot vineyard, where new practices were tested that were henceforth to become part of the production specifications for every grower in the cooperative. Grapes were picked while still unripe in August to reduce the number of bunches to five per vine plant, thereby cutting yields.

The actual harvesting took place when the red grapes were overripe. There was separate vinification for the various varieties. Temperature-controlled fermentation lasted from twenty to twenty-five days and wines were aged in barrels for a year in the château's *chais*.

The abbey of Saint-Mont was founded in 1050 in the village of Saint-Mont-Gers and belonged to the Order of Cluny, where the monks grew grapes and made wine. The influence of the monks on the development of the vine was so strong that the peasants were made to pay their taxes to them in the form of wine. The abbey has been classified as a historic monument and now belongs to Stéphane Lissner, director of the Centre International de la Création Théâtrale in Paris and director of the Festival d'Aix-en-Provence. It has been magnificently restored and the old cellars have been returned to their original use, that of aging wine. Vinification was entrusted to the Saint-Mont cooperative, which researched the historic location of the original plantings and, in honor of the memory of the monks, was able to re-create the monastery vineyard on the original plots with the help of several winemakers. The eighteen acres (seven hectares) of the old vineyard covered the slopes of the village (sometimes plots of only 3/4 acre [thirty hectares] had to be grouped together) and the result was a powerful wine—(14 percent alcohol for the Tannat variety)—with a dark, seductive appearance, a jammy nose, and a mouth of silky, velvety tannins.

The Château du Bascou is a pleasant nineteenth-century residence with a Picon tiled roof and picturesque half-timbering. The grounds contain old cedars and are ringed by a magnificent fifty acre (twenty hectare) vineyard, of which thirty acres (twelve hectares) are currently in production. The Producteurs Plaimont was shrewd enough to accentuate the typically Gascon style of the estate by aiding a couple of young winemakers to set up home there and offer high-quality hospitality. Four winemakers, in addition to working their own properties, use plots of land belonging to the château to conduct experiments that go further than those at Sabazan. The château, which only makes red Côtes de Saint-Mont, has become the pride of the appellation, as well as being a favorite vacation destination dedicated to the discovery of wine and its *terroirs*. Long neglected, this place has now been restored to its former glory. There are three guest rooms named for the grape varieties and a dining room where you can sample the local foods and taste the wines of the property. By complying with the new charter of the association, the vineyard meets the draconian requirements for classification in the *grands vins de Plaimont* category. The red is both complex and subtle, with an intense nose of berries, and a well-rounded flavor with harmonious tannins. Delicious!

By creating the Accueil Vignerons Plaimont network, the Producteurs Plaimont has introduced an original scheme whereby visitors can explore Gascon cuisine and wines by staying in a number of rural *gîtes* and guest rooms in winemaking properties, with the winemaker serving as guide. A number of events and celebrations provide a further reason to visit this region: the Vignoble en Fête in Saint-Mont in the spring; the famous Marciac jazz festival in the summer; the late harvest (*vendanges tardives*) and the auction of the *barriques d'or* at Pacherenc du Vic-Bilh in the autumn.

THE FIFTEENTH-CENTURY CHÂTEAU DE SABAZAN (FACING PAGE), ORIGINALLY A FORTIFIED FARMHOUSE, IS NOW A CHARMING GUEST HOUSE THAT PRIDES ITSELF ON ITS INFORMALITY, SERVING LOCAL DISHES AND WINES THAT HAVE BERRY AROMAS LACED WITH NOTES OF CLOVE AND CINNAMON. THE IROULÉGUY APPELLATION (BELOW) QUENCHES THE BASQUE COUNTRY THIRST WITH ITS DELICIOUS, HEARTY REDS AND LIVELY WHITES THAT SHOULD BE DRUNK YOUNG.

LANGUEDOC

A GOOD TIME TO VISIT MINERVOIS IS EARLY MAY,
WHEN THE VINE LEAVES FORM A BACKDROP TO THE MAGICAL
PURPLISH MIST OF THE FLAX FLOWERS, AS HERE NEAR THE VILLAGE
OF AIGNE, NOT FAR FROM MINERVE.

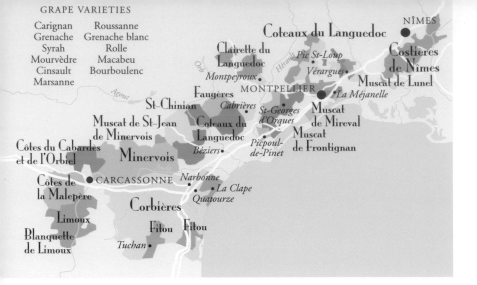

LANGUEDOC:
FROM LIMOUX TO NÎMES, A LAND OF SUN AND WIND

To explore the Languedoc is to explore a region that is raw, earthy, and powerful, exposed to extremes of climate, from burning sun to biting wind. This is a place where mountain and sea meet, a region of rocky spurs and ridges dotted with Cathar castles. There is an infinite variety of landscapes, from the *garrigue*, with its scents of thyme, lavender, rosemary, sage, and savory, to the vineyards, which are bathed in the fragrances of bay leaf, mint, thyme, and almond blossom, together with a hint of wild fennel and Aleppo pine. These smells intermingle and call to each other like a bouquet of echoes, from appellation to appellation.

In these beautiful if rebellious lands, in this land of winds and wine, no one says, "Shush, I'm tasting," because wine is shared and discussed, galvanizing the mind and the senses, in a spirit of fraternity. This is encapsulated by the cross of Languedoc on the neck of the bottle. Although of Christian origin, its twelve pommels symbolize the mastery of both the universe (the twelve astrological signs) and time (the twelve months of the year). It featured on the banners of the rulers of Languedoc, who took it East, and now, a thousand years later, it has become the rallying symbol and sign of recognition for all of the region's appellations.

We have not been able to consider all of the appellations, so we have just selected a few of them. May those we have had to leave out forgive us, because they all deserve to be tasted. It is hard to resist the Muscat de Lunel, for instance, the accompaniment to bull fights,

fougasse (the local bread), and carnivals. Its syrupy, aromatic depth is redolent of lemon and citrus, and as it ages it tastes of honey and dried fruits. And what can one say about the wine of Faugères, whose vineyards lie on the flanks of the Cévennes, arranged in south-facing terraces and whose yields are so small that it produces rounded, powerful wines with silky tannins that exhale the perfumes of ripe black currant and raspberry, of licorice and the *garrigue*, as the Cuvée Prestige of Château Les Estanilles illustrates so superbly.

Saint-Chinian, located between Espinouse and Caroux, flourishes in the heart of a landscape of mimosa and orange trees and is washed with the fragrances of the *garrigue*. Its fruity, smooth rosés are perfect accompaniments to ravioli, broiled fresh sardines, salads of octopus or squid, and the delicious cured meats of the neighboring Montagne Noire. The wines are supple, fruity, velvety, full of the aromas of licorice and of the *garrigue*. The reds offer magnificent alliances with steak in a thick red-wine sauce or broiled lamb Languedoc-style. As for the rich, deep, powerful wines that have made the reputation of Saint-Chinian, they are magnificent with beef stew, game, jugged wild boar, or spit-roasted hare. The white Picpoul de Pinet, whose vineyards run right down to the Thau lake, is drunk throughout the region as an accompaniment to fish, shellfish, and crustaceans. This mischievous wine is redolent of linden blossom and hawthorn and has a fresh taste, combining acidity and roundness.

THE SAINT-CHINIAN APPELLATION STRETCHES ACROSS THE ARID FOOTHILLS OF THE CÉVENNES IN THE HÉRAULT,
BETWEEN CESSENON-SUR-ORB AND FONTCAUDE. IT PRODUCES VIGOROUS REDS WITH DELIGHTFUL FRAGRANCES OF THE GARRIGUE:
BAY LEAVES, COOKED RED BERRIES, AND PRUNES, AS WELL AS MINERAL OR FRUITY ROSÉS THAT ARE A PERFECT MATCH FOR SALADS AND SUMMER BARBECUES.

And how can one convey that incredible view of the walled city of Carcassonne from the slopes of Cabardès, where both Atlantic and Mediterranean grape varieties are cultivated? Here, thanks to the winds from east and west, complex reds and rosés are bottled, with aromas of berries and tropical fruits that evolve, in the dark depths of wine cellars, into hints of tobacco, coffee, and prunes. Then there are the wines of maritime Fitou and continental Fitou, two children of the same appellation. The color of red madder, they have notes of carnation, bay leaf, and flintlock that combine well with stewed ceps, duck, or braised rabbit. Further inland are the vineyards of Limoux, which cover the slopes of the upper valley of the Aude and produce the famous Blanquette and Crémant de Limoux, together with wonderful and little-known dry wines with fragrances of apricot, apple, acacia, and hawthorn that are beginning to appear on prestigious wine lists. The terraced slopes of Malepère, bordered in the north by the Canal du Midi and in the east by the Aude, caught between Mediterranean and Atlantic influences, certainly

deserve a mention. In the triangle formed by Carcassonne, Limoux, and Castelnaudary, the microclimate is responsible for delicious reds and rosés which have deep, lively colors and aromas of fresh fruit. The young wines of the Côtes de Malepère express the scents of berries, strawberries, morello cherries, and black currant, developing notes of preserves, roasted coffee, brandied plums, truffles, and figs. As for the famous Muscat de Frontignan, which for the French recalls the sort of aperitifs drunk by their grandmothers, it has a topaz appearance, a flowery nose, and the fruity aromas of fresh grapes, pear, and citrus. There is not a single good *sommelier* who would not recommend this delicious wine for drinking with marzipan, lemon tarts, or fruit salads, since these combinations are almost legendary. In fact, according to legend, Hercules himself, wanting to finish the bottle to the last drop, twisted it forever into its present shape by using his fist.

This region is a huge amphitheater that backs onto the Cévennes, and is bounded by the Canigou, the Montagne Noire, the

foothills of the Alps, and the Spanish border. Strangely, its actual area has varied constantly over the centuries. Although it originally covered all the lands in which the Occitan language was spoken, it eventually shrank right down to the single county of Toulouse, then to the part once known as Bas Languedoc. Finally, in the minds of vacationers at least, it now consists of a carpet of sand stretching for nearly one hundred miles along the Mediterranean from Fitou to Aigues-Mortes. Dubbed "the French answer to California," the region of Languedoc-Roussillon is the largest vineyard in the world (733,000 acres [297,000 hectares]), accounting for one third of all French wines. It alone accounts for eighteen appellations, eleven of them still wines (Cabardès, Coteaux du Languedoc, Limoux, Minervois La Livinière, Clairette du Languedoc, Corbières, Fitou, Minervois, Faugères, Malepère, Saint-Chinian), four *vins doux naturels* (Muscat de Frontignan, Muscat de Mireval, Muscat de Lunel, Muscat de Saint-Jean-de-Minervois), and three sparkling wines (Blanquette de Limoux, Crémant de Limoux, and Blanquette Méthode Ancestrale).

Red wines represent 81 percent of wine production in the region, the rest being made up of rosés, sparkling wines, *vins doux naturels*, and other whites.

THE VINES COME RIGHT UP TO THE WALLS
OF THE MEDIEVAL TOWN OF CARCASSONNE (ABOVE),
SEEN HERE FROM THE PONT NEUF,
ABOVE THE BANKS OF THE AUDE.
NOT FAR FROM PAULIGNE, IN THE REGION OF LIMOUXIN,
A SEA OF VINES WASHES ACROSS THE HILLSIDES FROM
DOMAINE DE CASSAGNEAU (FOLLOWING DOUBLE PAGE).

47

CÔTEAUX DU LANGUEDOC:
AN EXCEPTIONAL TERROIR

Set against the spectacular backdrop of gorges, canyons, mountains, *garrigue*, and sandy beaches, this is the oldest vineyard in France. Praised by Pliny the Elder and Columella, it has been a magnet for the wealthy, from industrialists to movie stars, for the last fifteen years, all of them seeking the good life. This vast appellation, which radiates around the Golfe du Lion, touching the coastline at Narbonne in the west, the edge of the Camargue in the east, and resting against the foothills of the Montagne Noire and the Cévennes, contains a patchwork of *terroirs* and lifestyles of an incredible diversity. The statistics for the Languedoc are impressive. The appellation covers several *départements* and represents no fewer than 2,024 producers, eighty cooperative cellars and 398 privately owned estates. Production can be broken down into 78 percent red, 10 percent rosé, and 12 percent white, but the differences and characteristics of these wines are such that they have been grouped into twelve *terroirs*: La Clape, Cabrières, Saint-Saturnin, Montpeyroux, Saint-Georges-d'Orques, La Méjanelle, Saint-Christol, Saint-Drézéry, Pic Saint-Loup, Picpoul-de-Pinet, and Vérargues.

The *terroir* of La Clape, for example, has chalky soil, with warm, penetrating odors of pine trees that are caressed by sea breezes that tend to intoxicate rather than invigorate. On the terraces of Larzac, the vines are planted in crowded rows around Saint-Guilhem-le-Désert and up to the Pic Saint-Loup, famous for its huge cliff that dominates the vineyard, the most northerly in the Coteaux du Languedoc. A little further on, the vines of Sommières spread their untidy branches right up to the walls of Aigues-Mortes. The abbey of Valmagne, a Gothic edifice restored as a wine cellar, forms a contrast with the ostentatious châteaux on the plain, whose extravagantly neo-medieval styles advertise the great wealth that could be derived from extensive plantings of Aramon and Carignan.

For reds and rosés, the Grenache, Syrah, and Mourvèdre varieties represent at least half the blends, while Cinsault and Carignan are secondary varieties. This means that the red wines are velvety and elegant, with notes of raspberry, black currant, spices, and pepper when young; wines made for bottle aging develop notes of leather, bay leaf, and the fragrances of the *garrigue*, such as juniper, thyme, and rosemary. The fruity, spicy reds are wonderful accompaniments to the red mullet, sardines, tuna, and mackerel of the Mediterranean, the more mature wines working best with beef stew or preserved duck.

ITINERARY

In the village of Lavérune, which lies two and a half miles west of Montpellier, the vineyard of Saint-Georges-d'Orques, much admired by Rabelais, is hidden from view behind a magnificent seventeenth-century iron gate, once used to block off the Place de la Comédie in Montpellier. It is owned by the Château de l'Engarran, a magnificent eighteenth-century folly in the Régence style with a formal French garden that drops down terrace by terrace to a rockery fountain. The Grill family has lived here for five generations, but wine-growing and history have been intertwined here for the past three hundred years. Vine tendrils trail over the caryatids of the façade and the bestiary in the grounds, illustrating this shared destiny. This is an estate that has traditionally been run by women, and today the owners are the two daughters of Francine Grill, once a well-known figure in the area. In 1978 she pioneered the first estate-bottling in the whole of the Languedoc. From their 150 acres (60 hectares) of vines, the owners manage to make no fewer than eleven wines, one of them from a late harvesting. The richness of the *terroir*, similar to that of Châteauneuf-du-Pape, produces spicy,

IN 1820, CASKS MADE FROM RUSSIAN OAK WERE INSTALLED IN THE NAVE OF THE ABBEY OF VALMAGNE,
A MASTERPIECE OF CISTERCIAN ARCHITECTURE, TRANSFORMING IT INTO A SHRINE TO WINEMAKING. REDS, WHITES, AND ROSÉS
ARE AGED HERE, INCLUDING THE CUVÉE DE TURENNE, WINNER OF MANY GOLD MEDALS AND THE ESTATE'S FLAGSHIP WINE.

robust, and expressive wines that can be laid down for a long time. The great restaurants are well aware of this and you will find the wine lists of prestigious establishments such as L'Arpège, the Grand Véfour, and Paul Bocuse feature two of the estate's best wines, namely Adélys and Quetton-Saint-Georges. Diane Losfelt, the enologist and daughter of the house, is in charge of the blending and tries to respect the personality of each vintage. Generosity, balance, elegance, concentration, and smoothness give these wines a feminine finesse that is quite rare in the region.

The Château de Flaugergues is less than a mile from the center of Montpellier. It is the oldest of the Montpellier follies, the sort of *maison des champs* ("house in the fields") that notables built for themselves in the eighteenth century as country retreats. This beautiful historic monument is open to the public and is redolent of the authentic culture of the Languedoc. When visiting the château, guided by the owner himself, you will be amazed by an arched staircase that is unique in the world, built without any supporting pillar and rising three stories. Throughout the building, the history of art accompanies that of the vine. The place is a working winery, however, not just a tourist attraction, and the vines cover a *terroir* known as La Méjanelle in the Grès de Montpellier area, where vines and olive trees have been cultivated since Roman times. The ground is covered in round pebbles known as *grès*, vestiges of the Rhône delta, which give rise to a rich range of fine, aromatic wines. The Cuvée Colbert, selected from the best plots and aged in barrels, combines roundness, structure, and fruit, and is the best example of its kind. It is magnificent with broiled meats or a cheese platter.

The priory of Saint-Jean-de-Bébian is just under two miles from Pézenas, where the great French playwright Molière was born. The slopes form the foothills of the Cévennes. The property has retained numerous traces of the monks who first came here in the eleventh century, making it one of the oldest Romanesque chapels in the Languedoc. After the monks left, the estate was sold off as a national asset. Having taken over his family property in 1975, Alain Roux completely restructured the vineyard, planting noble varieties together with the traditional varieties used for making Châteauneuf-du-Pape. In 1994, wine writer Chantal Lecouty and Jean Claude Le Brun, former manager of the *Revue des vins de France*, a wine magazine, acquired this wonderful tool for making wine. The house, with its walls the color of crushed raspberries, has the air of a stud farm, and looks like an illustration from a design magazine. There are sixteenth-century ceilings, ageless walls, and Andalusian ceramics. The kitchen is red with gold polka dots and the reception room features an old bread oven. Everything here is an advertisement for the Midi and its lifestyle. The challenge that faced this unusual couple was that of producing great Mediterranean wines that were concentrated and suitable for aging. The seventy-seven acre (thirty-one hectare) vineyard is a patchwork of no fewer than forty plots, because only

VINES ON THE OUTSKIRTS OF VILLEVEYRAC, IN THE HÉRAULT (FACING PAGE). THE COTEAUX DU LANGUEDOC APPELLATION OFFERS AN UNEXPECTED DIVERSITY OF TERROIRS AND SOME DISTINGUISHED WINES, INCLUDING THE CUVÉE COLBERT MADE AT THE CHÂTEAU DE FLAUGERGUES AND THE WINES OF DOMAINE DE SAINTE-CROIX AND CHÂTEAU DE CALADROY (ABOVE).

the best *terroirs* were retained. The soils contain surprises. The white varieties were planted in soil containing 30 percent active limestone, the same percentage found in the great vineyards of Chablis or Meursault, so it is hardly surprising that the Prieuré Blanc, which is thick and smooth, is considered to be one of the finest wines in the South of France. The grapes are picked by hand, then sorted first in the vineyard and a second time at a table before being transferred to seventeenth-century stone vats. Each variety is vinified separately, and the wine is aged in barrels and bottled eighteen months after harvesting. In fact, if patience is a good counselor, it is also a perfect taster. That is because the red Prieuré wines, with their intense color and smooth texture, deserve to be forgotten for at least three or four years in a cellar. They can be enjoyed with fall dishes or exotic foods, such as caramelized pork or glazed duck. While waiting for them to mature, you can enjoy the second red wine of the house, known as La Chapelle, and the wonderful whites aged for between two and six years, which go well with white meats.

Leave the main road after a few rows of vines and follow the path lined with tall grass that zigzags up to the Château de Montpezat. Although the château is not open to the public, one can admire its Neo-Gothic architecture from the iron gate and the outbuildings that date from the sixteenth century. Montpezat is flanked by a high tower and stands in a magnificent park that contains an oak tree reputed to be over six hundred years old, as well as old plane trees and gigantic chestnut trees. Christophe Blanc, who farms his seventy-four acres (thirty hectares) organically, is a young winemaker who has managed to raise his estate to the forefront of the appellation. His wines, which he macerates for a minimum of thirty days, are fairly strong and built for aging. Yields are low and picking is done at night (grapes are sensitive to ultra violet light and to heat). This produces

highly sought after wines, especially as the wine guru Robert Parker has awarded very high grades to Montpezat. The white, consisting of 100 percent Sauvignon, is wonderful and is the estate's top wine together with La Pharaonne. The latter is aged in barrels and has aromas of berries and spices, making it the ideal companion for red meats and Moroccan stews. It is an excellent wine for laying down and can be forgotten in the wine cellar for a good ten years.

It took Gérard Bru, starting from nothing, twenty years to build an estate that has become a reference in the Languedoc. It all began in the 1980s when this industrialist from Montpellier decided to abandon his life as a businessman to dedicate himself to his passion for wine. Not far from the Pic Saint-Loup he bought around 125 acres (50 hectares) of land covered in *garrigue* and olive trees, where no vine had ever grown before. He spent many years clearing the land before he was able to plant, and rather than build a new home, he simply moved the former prefecture of Montpellier stone by stone to a new site perched on a hilltop in the village of Saint-Drézéry, bestowing on it the new name of Château Puech-Haut. Bru does nothing by halves, and in order to extract the best from this new *terroir* he hired Michel Rolland, one of the most talented enologists of Bordeaux. The winemaking installations look more like the huge *chais* of Médoc than those of the modest Languedoc appellation. The wine cellar is spectacular with its six hundred barrels sleeping under a vaulted, illuminated ceiling. The end product is certainly on a par with his ambitions and the wines produced here are spectacular. A tasting reveals wines with a strong personality (like their owner), but with great finesse, and wonderful fragrances of fruit and berries. The top red wine possesses all the qualities of a *grand cru*.

MINERVOIS: AMID THE FINEST WINES OF LANGUEDOC

Granted Appellation d'Origine Contrôlée status in 1985, Minervois is in a huge, natural amphitheater with a full southern exposure. Backed by the Montagne Noire, it stretches from the heights of Narbonne to the gates of Carcassonne, hugging the Canal du Midi in the south. Although the meadows of its low hills are fragrant with the scents of rockrose, rosemary, thyme, and groves of Aleppo pines, the plains are farmed and exposed fully to sun. The reds form the bulk of the wines made here, accounting for 96 percent of production, while the whites and rosés both account for only 2 percent. The red wines are well structured, supple, and elegant, with fragrances of black currant, violet, cinnamon, and vanilla. As they age, they develop notes of leather, preserved fruit, and prunes. The tannins are silky as well as full and long. The rosés are delicious when drunk young, with flavors of black currant and raspberry. They are lively in the mouth, developing in fullness and roundness. Depending on the *terroirs*, the whites may be fine, rounded, and persistent, enriched with the fragrances of tropical fruits and citrus, or they may be fresh, lively, and refreshing, exhaling floral fragrances of acacia and almond blossom. At the northeastern tip of the appellation, viscous white wines are produced that go by the name of Muscat de Saint-Jean-de-Minervois. The wine is straw-colored with pale green undertones and reflections, a little jewel that is redolent of just-picked grapes, acacia flowers, lemongrass, and citrus. This *vin doux naturel* is ideal as an aperitif or as an accompaniment to strong cheeses. It is very popular with the great restaurants and is only made by seven specialist cellars and one cooperative.

Minervois consists of a mosaic of terraces that descend in successive levels from the Montagne Noire right down to the Canal du Midi. These *terroirs*, consisting of terraces between 200 to 1,700 feet (50 to 500 meters) above sea level, are subject to wide variations of temperature. The climate is Mediterranean in the eastern part (Clamoux and Côtes Noires), since they are only about twenty miles from the sea, but the winters are quite harsh in the Causse, which is more than 1,000 feet (300 meters) above sea level.

La Livinière, an appellation within the appellation, is located at the heart of Minervois, in the *terroir* of the Petit Causse. It is sheltered by steep slopes, bordered on the west by the Serre d'Oupia, famous for its windmills, and constitues an exceptional *terroir*, which is why its boundaries are strictly marked and it is classified separately. It covers 655 acres (265 hectares), and is made by thirty-four producers and six cooperatives. The appellation covers six villages in the *département* of the Hérault and one in the Aude. Although these vineyards were originally recognized as part of the Minervois appellation, a rigorous development strategy resulted in their recognition as an entirely separate *cru* in 1999. Aromatic complexity and concentration is what makes these wines outstanding. They develop fragrances of black currant, the *garrigue*, and black olives that develop into notes of leather. They are very full in the mouth, being fat and full of elegant tannins, which benefit from being laid down for five to eight years.

ITINERARY

Situated at the northwestern tip of the appellation, Château Villerambert-Julien has a magnificent entrance lined with blue irises. The name comes from the Latin Villa Ramberti and the property was built on a very old site surrounded by ancient standing

THE LEGENDARY WALLED VILLAGE OF MINERVE WITH ITS VENERABLE ARCHED BRIDGE
HAS LENT ITS NAME TO THE MINERVOIS APPELLATION. WITH ITS 11,000 ACRES (4,500 HECTARES)
OF VINES, THE APPELLATION HAS BEEN A PROMISED LAND FOR MANY AN ASPIRING PRODUCER.

stones, dolmens, and menhirs, close to the Via Domitia. Although it is first mentioned in chronicles in 1231, the château in its present form was only built in the sixteenth century. In 1858, it was bought by the Julien family, who sensitively restored it, the last restoration being the little vaulted chapel of the château that now houses the wine-tasting room. A lectern and the head of an angel are reminders of the origin of this place, which is rather somber in appearance. The only concession in this purity is the wrought-iron balustrade of the staircase, a whirl of arabesques, which can be admired while tasting the estate's top wine, its rosé. This brightly colored vintage has become a classic and comes from the most aromatic vats. It is powerful but has a lovely nose of crushed berries which develops into grapefruit, as well as a consistent flavor without artificial aromas or dry finish. In short, a truly drinkable rosé. As for the red wine, it has aromatic complexity and silky tannins that place it among the best wines of the appellation. The single *terroir* of Villerambert-Julien consists of eleven soil types, one of which, a very specific one, consists of marble. At the northern end of the property, the grinding up of veins of pink marble has made it possible to create a vineyard that is almost unique in the world. Only Grenache has survived here, giving concentrated wine. Before leaving the estate, make sure you visit the little museum located beneath the offices, where old wine making equipment is exhibited in a very nostalgic setting.

Nearby Château de Violet is a timeless edifice with a charm that defies categorization. It is a combination of winemaking property, delightful hotel, and little museum devoted to wine—and vinegar—making. The whole enterprise is skillfully run by a lively widow who bought the château in 1963 and who carries her eighty summers lightly. The château, the foundations of which date from the tenth century, was modified in the seventeenth and nineteenth centuries. It stands on the site of a Gallo-Roman villa. The wine cellar sates from the eighteenth century and there is a delightful little gourmet food shop. As part of the hotel operation, Émilie organizes wine-tasting courses and "discovery weekends" centered around wine. Her white wine known as La Dame Blanche is fresh and well worth tasting and it has won a number of medals since 1991. She is also proud of her Clovis.

Take a leisurely walk from the village of Siran to Centeilles past cypress trees, wild almonds, heather, lavender, and thyme. After following the low walls of schist enclosing the vines that are reminiscent of Burgundy, you reach the Clos de Centeilles. It is located a stone's throw from a lovely thirteenth-century church. In 1990, Daniel Domergue, a former bookseller from Montpellier, decided to settle here with his wife and their five children. It took them thirteen

For nearly fifty miles, the Canal du Midi passes through vineyards whose grapes are used to make Minervois, vins de pays, and, as here at Capestang, a village near Béziers, vins de table.

years of hard work to transform the estate into what it is today. The handsome house, built of fieldstone, is reached through a large gateway, looking worthy and proud of its great age. There is a brand new kitchen presided over by an old-fashioned cook and floor tiles that are ungrouted. As for the rest, it is a home that looks lived in, with an air of make-do-and-mend, but it clearly has aristocratic forebears. As for the vineyard, it flows in terraces across thirty-five acres (fourteen hectares), with a fully southern exposure in which all the varieties of the appellation are represented. Most of the stocks are between twenty and fifty years of age, and the Carignan vines are as old as eighty. The ancient traditions are respected for plowing, pruning, trimming, and hand-picking. Maceration is very slow—taking four to eight weeks—the basis of the successful alchemy of these wines. Five reds are made here, each with a distinctive personality. They are aged in enameled vats to avoid the wine acquiring the taste of the wood. The Campagne de Centeilles is made mainly with Cinsault grapes from old stock. Carignanissime, made from low-yielding Carignan grapes, shows to what extent, where the geological and cultural conditions are just right, this ancient, much decried variety becomes rich and spicy. As for the Capitelle de Centeilles, which takes it names from the drystone shepherd's hut, it is a pure Cinsault, which speaks eloquently of youth. It has a lovely color containing shades of mauve and fruity aromas, and is sharp in the mouth. It is a lively wine that is frank and honest, recalling the flavors of a Chirouble or a Juliénas. Finally, there is the Clos Centeilles. This elegant Languedoc blend has a nose of black berries, mild spices, cedarwood, and licorice, with deep, powerful tannins. It is the ideal wine to accompany the finest cuts of meat.

Upon returning to the village, you must stop at the Ostal Cazes, where the famous owner of the Château Lynch Bage, Jean-Michel Cazes from Bordeaux, has beautifully restored an old tile-making factory into a tasting room. Lovers of the good and the beautiful can buy the great Circus wine here, a very well-made *vin de pays* with a red and gold label.

The Canal du Midi has been classified by UNESCO as a World Heritage site, and is an excellent means for traveling from east to west across the Minervois appellation. It runs for around forty-five miles, interspersed with locks, weirs, and ports. Since 1996, the Port-Minervois port authority at Homps, which is installed in a former nineteenth-century wine merchant's store beside the canal, has acted as the showcase for the winemakers of the region. The store, known as the "Chai," is decked out to look like something from the days when wine was sold by the barrel, and offers more than a 140 different wines from seventy estates in the appellation. Once a week, a winemaker offers a tasting and talks about his work. A major event is held at the quay in mid-June when all the winemakers get together for a festive evening organized around their wines. Come see it before you drink.

A houseboat, a popular mode of transportation for tourists, makes it possible to moor at the landing of the Château de Bassanel. This huge eighteenth-century property is built on a steep slope in the east of the appellation. It has 153 acres (62 hectares) of vines and 172 acres (70 hectares) of *garrigue*. The huge iron entrance gates open onto a dry, stony vineyard of ancient, sun-baked vines, large umbrella pines, arbutus trees, and even a small olive grove. For land-lubbers, the charms of this little property can be discovered starting from its little chapel with its stone lacework façade, where all that is celebrated today is the cult of Dionysos. The red wine made here has a heady, generous fragrance and a lovely velvety crimson color, with a deep, silky mouthfeel. With its strength, fine flavor of wild bay leaf, vigorous sap of balsamic essences, pure and heavy odor of damp earth, and velvety texture of sun-scorched stone, the Château de Bassanel is indeed worthy of a Mass.

COSTIÈRES DE NÎMES:
AN APPELLATION TO BE EXPLORED

Not yet Provence and not quite part of Occitanie, Costières de Nîmes lies to the south and east of the city that has given its name to the appellation, between the Languedoc and the Rhône valley. The *autoroute du soleil* and the N86, roads familiar to legions of vacationers in France, help to form the boundaries of this small winemaking region bordered in the east by the Rhône canal, in the south by the N113, and in the north by the river Gard. The vineyard is shaped like an elongated trapezium, and lies in the heart of one of France's most popular tourist regions. It covers an area delimited by Meynes, Jonquières, Saint-Vincent, and Beaucaire northeast of Nîmes, and by Saint-Gilles, Vauvert, and the Camargue in the south.

The presence of the mistral, the keen northern wind, is as important as the geology of the *terroir*. The land is covered with alluvial pebbles that were washed down from the Alpine glaciers and rounded by the Rhône and Durance rivers. The roots of the vines are forced to forge a passage between the stones, going down a long way in a search for food and water. That is one of the reasons why the wines of Costières de Nîmes are so pure and fragrant. These deep roots absorb a quantity of minerals that contribute to the complex composition of the grapes. Another advantage of these pebbly soils is that the act like a thermostat, maintaining the temperature of the soil during the day and storing heat, which they release at night.

The weather is beneficial here, with record amounts of sunshine and warm temperatures. But although the climate of the appellation is Mediterranean, the northern wind that blows down from the Alps, the famous mistral, also has a beneficial effect on the vines. By blowing away parasites and drying the rows of vines after the rains, it also prevents the formation of fungal growth.

Even though other *terroirs* claim to have found favor with the Greeks, those claims are particularly justified here. The discovery of an amphora-making workshop near Beaucaire attests to the importance of the wine trade in the Gallo-Roman period. During the Middle Ages, the abbey of Saint-Gilles even had the privilege of delivering wine to the popes at their residence in Avignon. In the late nineteenth century, however, the phylloxera plague struck, destroying the vines. As a response to this disaster, the vines were no longer grown on the slopes but planted on the richer plains. Although production increased, quality declined. It was above all thanks to the efforts of Philippe Lamour that the appellation adopted a policy of renewal. New varieties were planted, the *terroir* was studied, and the *chais* were modernized. It was a true renaissance. Consequently, in 1950, Costières du Gard became a Vin Délimité de Qualité Supérieure, and in 1986 it was upgraded to an Appellation d'Origine Contrôlée. Three years later, in a unique move for an appellation, the name was changed to Costières de Nîmes, thus restoring the traditional name of the hills on which the vines are grown.

Contrary to many other appellations, a bottle from this appellation can be identified at a glance due to its very distinctive appearance. This has been dubbed "Nîmoise," and features the name of the appellation, together with the new logo of the city of Nîmes showing a crocodile at the foot of a palm tree, which was created by designer Philippe Starck.

Costières, the youngest appellation in the Rhône valley, is made in three colors. These sunny, easy-drinking wines should on the whole be enjoyed within two or three years of the harvest.

The red wines are distinctive and harmonious, well rounded and generous. They are characterized by aromas of berries and soft fruits such as plums or cherries. When young they make excellent

AT THE MAS DES TOURELLES IN BEAUCAIRE, TOGAS AND WICKER PANNIERS AWAIT THE PICKERS WHO GATHER
THE GRAPES USED TO RECREATE THE FAMOUS TRILOGY OF ROMAN WINES—MULSUM, CARENUM,
AND TURRICULAE. TURRICULAE, WHICH HAS AN AROMA OF WALNUTS, CONTAINS SEAWATER.

table companions to broiled or grilled meats. When aged, they go well with braised meats in sauce and with cheeses. Carignan offers structure and wonderful color, but only when the wine is aged. Grenache contributes high alcoholic content, bouquet, and robustness. Mourvèdre is used for its tannins and berry fragrances, and Syrah for its aromatic qualities.

The rosés are full, delicate, and delicious, with tones of berries and dried fruits. Light and fresh in the mouth, they demand to be drunk young and are perfect as an aperitif or with white meat. Harmonious and balanced, they are every shade of pink from pale rose to grenadine, the equivalent of a basket of summer fruit. They are made from a blend of Cinsault, used for its finesse, combined with Syrah or Grenache.

The white wines, which are not well known to the general public, have floral and fruity notes and a pale color. They express roundness, suppleness, and silkiness through notes of citrus and soft fruit. They are delicious with broiled or grilled fish and soft goat cheese. Although the white wines are mostly made from a blend of Grenache Blanc, with smaller amounts of Marsanne and Roussanne, such varieties as Clairette, Bourboulenc, Macabeu, and Rolle are also used.

ITINERARY

The Château de la Tuilerie is one of the most important stops in the Costières region, and is the best-known château in the appellation, appearing frequently in the French media. It has been owned by the same family for three generations, and is run by Chantal and Pierre-Yves Comte, who see themselves as "artisans of the vine." The former sheepfold of this nineteenth-century château has been converted into a store-cum-tasting room called the Jardin des Vins (the wine garden). It sells wines from the château, superb brandies, and very old rum from Martinique, where the owner's family settled thirty years ago. Particularly attractive is the series of "romantic cuvées" to celebrate Valentine's Day, with theme titles such as Bisous, Notes de Cœur, Câlins, and Cuvée des Amours.

The red Cuvée des Amours has a nose of fresh mulberries and violets that is perfect with roast or broiled meats and vegetable gratins. The white version is gold-green in color and has a nose of white flowers, brandy, and brioche. It is a worthy companion to broiled fish, shellfish, and goat cheese. The Sarments and Carte Blanche ranges deserve a special mention, as do the Dînettes et Croustilles wines that are sold in half-liter bottles, ideal for *tête-à-têtes*.

The Château de Valcombe lies closer to the heart of the appellation, in the *commune* of Générac, with a vineyard facing south. The château overlooks the village of Saint-Gilles about two miles away, which is famous for its abbey, the second-largest in Europe. The driveway consists of an avenue over half a mile long of cypresses and pines that are more than 250 years old. It was used as a location for a scene in the movie *Les Enfants du siècle*, starring Juliette Binoche. The château itself has a classical charm, with white shutters that are often closed. It was acquired by the present owner's family in 1730, but is only used as a vacation home. The tasting room is installed in the former stables, where the manger and flooring made of local Costières stone have been retained, as have the brick-colored ceramic tiles that were once used to line the vats. Here vinification is meticulously handled. For the Cuvée Prestige, the final blending and bottling does not take place until ten to twelve months after harvesting. The result is a dark, rich, complex wine that has delicious fragrances of jammy fruit. It deserves to be forgotten for a few years in the wine cellar. The Garance, which comes in a special bottle with a deep punt, is made from 95 percent Syrah, and stays for thirteen to fifteen months in oak barrels. Its garnet color with its deep reflections is very attractive, and it has extraordinary aromatic complexity, with a smoky, toasted quality and a pronounced note of vanilla. With its three-hundred-year-old plantings of Syrah, Valcombe is justifiably proud of its status as one of the oldest wineries in the South of France, as is demonstrated by the medals won at the world's fairs of 1855 and 1873 that are proudly displayed on the walls of the wine-tasting room.

For more than 250 years, the Mas des Tourelles has been a family property classified as Costières de Nîmes, Vin de Pays d'Oc, and Vin de Pays du Gard. The property is located in the extreme southeast corner of the appellation and is surrounded by large, vigorous olive trees, cypresses, and almond and fig trees. A pomegranate tree stands next to the beautiful blood-colored rosé farmhouse, which is appropriately named Les Grenades ("the pomegranates"). A two-hundred-year-old wisteria clads the property and has also given its name to one of the wines, La Cour des Glycines. In a display that is both educational and attractive, a life-size reconstruction has been created of a Gallo-Roman wine cellar with a wooden lever press, grape-treading vat, and fermentation jars. During the harvest, which takes place on the second Sunday in September, the hand-picked grapes are trodden by grape-pickers dressed in togas. The wines are made using the ancient Roman techniques described in the treatise on agriculture written by Cato the Censor, the writings of the famous naturalist Pliny the Elder, and those of Lucius Columella. In 1991, this *mas* located a short distance from the Via Domitia, the ancient road that linked Italy with Spain, began cultivating two and a half acres (one hectare) of "archaeological wines" because a Gallo-Roman villa with an estate of seven acres (three hectares) stood on exactly the same spot. In addition to the villa and farmland, there was also a pottery. A campaign of archaeological digs began in 1980 and unearthed five huge kilns, in which as many as two thousand amphorae a day could be baked.

A favorite drink in Roman times was Mulsum, a combination of wine, honey, plants, and spices such as cinnamon, pepper, and

THE WINDSWEPT LANDSCAPES OF CORBIÈRES (FACING PAGE), REVEAL THE FLAVORS OF AN INFINITY OF TERROIRS, ON WHICH VINEYARDS AND OLIVE GROVES MAKE COMMON CAUSE. THE RUGGED, WINDSWEPT TERRAIN OF CORBIÈRES IS HOME TO BOTH VINES AND OLIVE TREES. THE STABLES OF THIS FORMER COACHING INN CONTAIN CASKS BOUGHT SECONDHAND FROM THE BORDEAUX REGION (RIGHT). THEY ARE USED TO AGE THE WINES OF MAS NEUF AND OTHER BLENDS IN THE COSTIÈRES DE NÎMES, INCLUDING CHÂTEAU DE VALCOMBE'S GARANCE AND MOURGUES DU GRÈS'S TERRE D'ARGENS (FAR RIGHT).

LEFT: THE ENTRANCE GATE OF THE MAS NEUF. THE WINES OF THIS PROPERTY, WHICH WAS ONCE A STAGE ON THE PILGRIMS' ROUTE TO THE SHRINE OF SANTIAGO DE COMPOSTELA, REGULARLY WIN MEDALS AND ARE DISTINGUISHED BY THEIR SUPERB BALANCE AND GREAT FINESSE.
FACING PAGE: A BUNCH OF GRAPES JUST BEFORE HARVESTING. THIS VARIETY CAN PRODUCE FINE WINES RICH IN FLORAL AROMAS AND LOW IN ACIDITY.

thyme. Today, this sweet drink goes wonderfully with spicy foods, blue cheese, or a chocolate dessert. Turriculae is proof that the Romans also enjoyed dry wines. The fermentation process was arrested by adding seawater, fenugreek, and *defructum* (grape juice concentrated by boiling) during vinification. Carenum is a sweet wine obtained by fermenting very ripe grapes with plants, quince, and *defructum*, and its praises were sung by Palladius. This unctuous amber wine with its aromas of peach preserves and caramel makes an original accompaniment to foie gras or fruit tart. Before leaving this estate that has been transformed into a center for historical research, make sure you visit the Roman garden, where cypresses and olive trees serve as the backdrop for a *lucus*, the sacred grove that the Romans used to create in the vicinity of their villas.

To reach Mourgues du Grès, star of the appellation and the neighboring property to Les Tourelles, you must leave the main road from Bellegarde and take the long and well-worn road that runs beside lush orchards and evergreen oaks. After having negotiated a few too many ruts, you finally reach the courtyard of this eighteenth-century farmhouse with almond green shutters, where a sundial carved into the wall like a symbol bears the inscription *Sine Sole Nihil* (Nothing without the Sun). The brightly lit reception room for guests is furnished with Provençal furniture and a venerable grand piano. Comfortable sofas have been placed around an old fireplace, where you can relax while tasting some of the magnificent wines. The estate covers about one hundred acres (forty hectares) grouped together on a southern slope. François Collard, an engineer, agronomist, and enologist with the reputation of being the star pupil of the appellation, makes his wine in the traditional way, seeking balance, fruit, and concentration. He learned his trade at Château Lafite-Rothschild, but then went into journalism. He decided to become a winemaker after taking over the family estate, which he transformed into one of the

top names of the appellation. Capable of surprising the most jaded of palates, the wines of this estate have aromas of the *garrigue*, black olives, fruit, and aromatic herbs. The winemaker believes that nothing should be allowed to interfere with the flavor of the fruit, so whites are fermented in stainless steel vats and the reds in concrete vats. Thus, in the wonderful wine known as Les Galets Rouges, a blend of Syrah, Grenache, and a touch of Mourvèdre, the nose expresses notes of black olives, bay leaves, spices, and licorice. In the mouth, it has great finesse underpinned by soft tannins. The whites should not be missed either. The Terre d'Argence, dominated by Roussanne with a hint of Grenache Blanc, has a full nose of dried apricots, violets, broom, and honey. A delight!

Finally, here is a piece of gossip. For those parishioners who are curious to know what wines the clergy like to use to celebrate Mass, the abbey of Notre-Dame-des-Neiges at Saint-Laurent-les-Bains has just launched its own Costières de Nîmes wine. The abbey specializes in making sacramental wine, and has produced a wine according to the rules of canon law called Ictus. A true miracle for the appellation.

CORBIÈRES:
A MOSAIC OF TERROIRS

When the Pyrenees were formed during the Paleozoic era, the Corbières region acquired a few wrinkles that are now the reason for its charm. These geological shenanigans produced grandiose landscapes of high mountains and wild valleys, which are now in the Aude *département*. Bordered to the east by the Mediterranean Sea, to the west by the first slopes of the Pyrenees, to the north by Minervois, and to the south by the Fitou appellation, the Corbières region forms a rhomboid bounded by the cities of Carcassonne, Narbonne, Perpignan, and Quillan. The majestic scenery is dotted with Cathar fortresses, Cistercian abbeys, Romanesque chapels, and farmhouses in the local style. It is windswept and sun-beaten, and much loved by tourists. Yet the district is defined largely by the vine.

The Corbières appellation is the largest vineyard in the Languedoc-Roussillon region, and the fourth-largest in France in terms of volume. Red wine accounts for 95 percent of its production, rosés 3.5 percent, and white wines 1.5 percent. There are forty cooperatives, which produce almost two-thirds of the output, and 332 individual estates. The territory is so vast that there are considerable differences between wines made from grapes grown beside the Mediterranean and those produced on the high terraces in the southwest. As for the soil, limestone alternates with shale, volcanic rock, and sand. Eleven different *terroirs* have been identified, although the winemakers of Corbières tend to reduce these to seven or eight different types of wine. The influence of the Mediterranean and the keen winds that blow in from the Atlantic, even managing to cross the Montagne d'Alaric, create a very specific climate resulting in red wines that are more vigorous and concentrated than those of Minervois, where the summer is not as dry.

One of the most highly regarded *terroirs* is Boutenac, which has recently acquired the status of *cru*, bearing the designation Appellation Corbières Boutenac Contrôlée. The *terroir* consists of a succession of low hills, devoid of other vegetation, that are very favorable to the aromatic expression of the Carignan variety. The reds produced here are considered to be the best in Corbières. They have a deep garnet or ruby color, with a nose of berries, spices, and thyme, and silky, melting tannins. The whites made here are ample and long, with a floral nose and aromas of vanilla and brioche. As for the rosés, they are fruity and floral.

Then there is the *terroir* of Durban, ringed by a rocky barrier, and rising to a height of 600 meters (2,000 feet). It is made up of a mosaic of little plots perched on the slopes. The reds here are robust and long-lived, the rosés are light and fruity, and the whites are dry, aromatic, and tasty. Next to the Durban *terroir* is that of Sigean along the coast, which has a clay and limestone soil.

The Hautes Corbières is made up of three *terroirs*—Quéribus, Saint-Victor, and Termenès—and cover an area of 8,400 acres (3,400 hectares), of which more than 2,500 acres (1,000 hectares) are classified as Appellation d'Origine Contrôlée. In Quéribus, the cherry-colored or vermilion wines have a full nose of raspberry and black currant ending in cocoa and roasted coffee. In Saint-Victor, the reds are rich, generous, and rounded, and on the heights of Termenès—the highest *terroir* in Corbières—they are very ample, with notes of spices, developing into the fall fragrances of undergrowth and truffles. This high *terroir* also produces the most brilliant whites of the appellation.

Then there is Fontfroide, a *terroir* that has been blessed by the gods, separated from the coast by a small mountain chain. Its warm, dry climate is paradise for the Mourvèdre variety. Despite its cardinal red color, this is not a truly sacramental wine, but it does have a delicious nose of red berries that develops spicy notes.

The *terroir* of Lagrasse is located in an another inspired valley, at between 500 and 800 feet (150 and 250 meters) above sea level on

the lands of a Carolingian abbey. It is somewhat sheltered from the scorching summer sun by the Montagne d'Alaric. The red wines here are particularly likeable, their ruby color enriched with amber tints. They are very aromatic, long in the mouth, elegant, and refined.

The *terroir* of Lézignan, which occupies a broad ledge less than twenty miles from the sea, produces sturdy reds dominated by fragrances of pepper and the *garrigue*.

The *terroir* of Serviès occupies a depression that is closed off at the northern end by the Montagne d'Alaric, and benefits from both Mediterranean and continental climatic influences. The Syrah variety reigns supreme here and produces ruby red, elegant wines, whose floral fragrances are most noticeable when they are young. Finally there is the *terroir* of the Montagne d'Alaric, where the soil is made up of clay and chalk and the vines are cultivated on terraces.

In short, although a single appellation, Corbières contains a mosaic of different soil types and climatic influences, something that is true of the whole of the Languedoc-Roussillon region.

The main grape varieties used are Grenache, Syrah, Mourvèdre, Cinsault, and above all Carignan, which is at its best in this region, to the point almost of being a guarantor of good quality. These varieties are typical of the Southwest and offer winemakers the opportunity of producing red *vins de garde*, with spicy fragrances dominated by notes of the *garrigue*, leather, and roasted coffee. The white wines of Corbières are blended mainly from the Grenache Blanc, Bourboulenc, Macabeu, Marsanne, and Roussanne varieties.

ITINERARY

She was a dress designer for Dior, he was an adviser to the director of the INSEE, the French national institute of statistics. Fed up with life in Paris, they went in search of a vineyard attached to a property with character, close to a vacation destination. After a year of searching, they discovered Château Prieuré Borde-Rouge and fell in love with it. Despite the enormous amount of work that they knew it would require, Natacha and Alain Devillers-Quenehen bought this domaine in 1994. The property is located on the lands that belonged to the abbey of Lagrasse in the Middle Ages, when it was reputed for producing the finest reds of the appellation, and takes its name from the particularly red vein of clay-and-limestone soil in this area and from the place name of "la Borde," which means "the farm" in the Occitan language. The building was once a priory, small farm, and dwelling, and parts are extremely old. The kitchen, for example, dates from 900. In the summer, a tasting room is opened in the *chais*. A welcoming setting is created: tables covered with linen tablecloths are set up among the barrels, and soft sofas and low tables await the visitors who come to taste the wine. Visitors are free to wander anywhere at Borde-Rouge—in the garden, the drawing room, the pergola, or under the cherry trees and plum trees, whose branches extend beside the impeccably pruned vines. Before it got to look like this, the vineyard was reconfigured, reshaped, and replanted, in order to be able to produce its hand-crafted *cuvées*.

Although the owners are proud of their white wine aged in vats and vinified like a Burgundy, the finest wine of the estate is indisputably the Ange, in homage to the owner's collection. Only three thousand bottles are made of this wine, which is aged for eighteen months in oak casks. Since the quality of wines depends very much on the quality of the people who make them, you can visit Borde-Rouge at any time of day and be sure of a warm welcome. For those who would like to extend their stay, there is also a guest house with two rooms.

Even for people with a good sense of direction, Château de Pech-Latt is hard to find. To get there, you have to leave the road that climbs into the mountains at Ribaute, pass through the little village with its chaotic, narrow streets, then find a track after the bridge that involves more climbing. Eventually you will glimpse the imposing but rather grim edifice flanked by a large tower. At the entrance there is a rusty old windmill, and you park in the huge farmyard, shaded by plane trees, acacias, and cherry trees, and where bright red roses climb over the thick, austere walls. From this vantage point, you can admire the rows of vines, the village of Ribaute, and the valley of the Orbieu to the east. Pech-Latt is located in the *terroir* of Lagrasse, and has been growing grapes organically since 1991. The estate, which once belonged to monks, has been making wines since the twelfth century. In the nineteenth century, a distant cousin of French composer Hector Berlioz bought the house, which is currently owned by a Burgundian. The twelfth-century cellar is contemporaneous with the abbey and has preserved its ancient vats, which are beautifully patinated with age. The ancient wine presses serving as a bar counter, the stools made of pine trunks, and a hand wine press in the center of the room all add a note of old-fashioned charm, but you only have to taste the three red wines, including the superb Alix, in order to understand to what extent Pech-Latt has moved into the present. A biodynamic approach is adopted here, ensuring low yields for optimum quality. The grapes harvested are exceptional and the resulting wines delicious.

The Château de Luc is located at the entrance to the village of Luc-sur-Orbieu. The porch on the left leads to the back of the château; on the right there is the huge *chai*. You reach the tasting cellar by a little staircase. Upon entering, you will notice a fragment of a sarcophagus dating from the sixth century, the time of the Merovingians, which sets the tone. After tasting the splendidly robust and spicy reds and admiring the château's ceremonial courtyard, magnificent seventeenth-century main door, and eighteenth-century windows, you should ask to see the wine cellar, entered via a wide staircase of worn stone. Nothing seems to have changed for

IN CORBIÈRES, THE ARCHITECTURAL AND WINEMAKING HERITAGES ARE SOMETIMES INTERTWINED. THE ABBEY OF FONTFROIDE (PRECEDING PAGE) IS ALSO THE NAME OF SOME REFINED WINES. THE RED HAS NOTES OF FENNEL AND THYME, WHILE THE WHITE IS REDOLENT OF WHITE-FLESHED FRUITS.
IN THE SEVENTEENTH-CENTURY CELLAR OF THE CHÂTEAU D'ORMESSON AT LÉZIGNAN (BELOW), UNDER THE PAYS D'OC LABEL, REDS, WHITES, AND ROSÉS ARE VINIFIED, OF WHICH THE FINEST VINTAGES ARE MARKETED UNDER THE NAME ENCLOS D'ORMESSON.

centuries here. Old bottles lie in rows that stretch far back into the darkness and dust, and there is the characteristic odor, both acrid and vinous, of old cellars that is a delight to the eyes and fires the imagination. The property has 123 acres (50 hectares) of vines, of which 50 percent are old Carignan, 30 percent Syrah, and 20 percent Grenache. Louis Fabre, father of five children, is the winemaker. He took over the family property in 1982 and runs it with the help of his sister. The estate's wines have excellent depth of flavor. They are made from grapes that have reached a state of complete ripeness, but a lot of hard work is done in the cellars in order to retain maximum fruitiness. In this family, although wine has been made for fourteen generations, this is the first generation to do its own bottling. This is an example of the illustrious past of Corbières wine and also the promise of a great future.

ROUSSILLON

On the steep slopes facing the Mediterranean,
two AOCs are produced from neighboring vines,
the very recent Coullioure and the classic Banuyls.

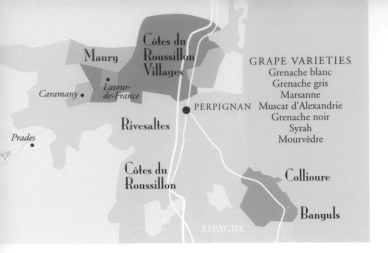

ROUSSILLON:
WINES FULL OF FRUIT AND SUGAR

Roussillon is more of a secret than a region, a place that for too long France has for overlooked and considered as a provincial backwater. It is a place with a head for heights, lounging comfortably between Mont Canigou (altitude 6,000 feet [1,800 meters]) in the west, the Albères mountain range in the south, and the rugged hills of Corbières in the north. As a region, it is poised at the very edge of France, hence the strong influence of neighboring Catalonia. It is cooled by both the tramontane winds of the Pyrenees and sea breezes from the Mediterranean, and thus has the driest and sunniest climate in the whole of France. It forms the eastern section of the *département* of Pyrénées-Orientales, and with its 2,500 hours of sunshine per year, it is perfectly suited for growing grapes. Vines can be found all over the immense plain that stretches along the coastline, carpeting the hills, leapfrogging the colorful little ports, milling around the brick-built houses surrounded by umbrella pines, and living happily alongside the almond trees, olive trees, mimosa, lavender, and rosemary.

To gain an idea of the importance of the Roussillon vineyards, it should be realized that the *département* of Pyrénées-Orientales is the second most productive French *département* in terms of volume of wine made, and that it produces 90 percent of the country's *vins doux naturels*. The region has twelve Appellations d'Origine Contrôlées, including five for *vins doux naturels* (Banyuls, Banyuls Grand Cru, Maury, Muscat de Rivesaltes, and Rivesaltes) and three for dry wines (Collioure, Côtes-du-Roussillon, Côtes-du-Roussillon Villages). An additional designation

has been created for this final group of wines, Côtes-du-Roussillon Villages, which also bears the name of the *commune*: CRV Caramany, CRV Latour de France, CRV Lesquerde, and CRV Tautavel. There are also countless *vins de pays*, such as those of the Pyrénées-Orientales and the Catalan coast. The locals adopt a more simple schema: for them, the dessert wines are Banyuls wines and the dry whites are Collioure wines.

VINS DOUX NATURELS

The region's *vins doux naturels*—sweet wines fortified with grape spirit—were the first in France to be granted Appellation d'Origine Contrôlée status. Even the great Roman writer Pliny the Elder remarked on their quality. Rivesaltes Ambré is generally made from Grenache Blanc and Gris or Macabeu and is deep gold in color. It has a flavor of almonds, hazelnuts, citrus preserves, and coffee, and goes well with Moroccan dishes such as the pigeon pie known as *b'stilla* and *tajine*. Rivesaltes Grenat is made from Grenache Noir and is bottled young. If the wine is aged in barrels and in contact with the air for less than two years, it is known as Rivesaltes Tuilé, due to its tile-red color with hints of brown or orange. Tuilé wines develop aromas of coffee, cocoa, tobacco, and fig or plum jam. They make wonderful dessert wines and go especially well with fruit tarts. Finally, Rivesaltes Hors d'Âge is different again from Ambré and Tuilé because it is aged for a minimum of five years. It is a

THE VINEYARDS OF ROUSSILLON ARE BORDERED BY THE SEA IN THE EAST, THE PYRENEES IN THE SOUTH,
AND THE HILLS OF CORBIÈRES IN THE NORTH. THE TERRAIN FORMS A VAST AMPHITHEATER,
WITH THE CITY OF PERPIGNAN AS THE AUDIENCE AND THE GREAT MONT CANIGOU CENTER STAGE.

delight to drink at the end of a good meal. Muscat de Rivesaltes is produced from two varieties of grape, the Muscat of Alexandria and Muscat à Petits Grains ("small grape Muscat"). The former provides the wine with depth, the aromas of ripe fruit, and the fragrance of blossoms; the latter contains the flavors of tropical fruit, citrus, candy, or sorbets. This wine is the ideal accompaniment for perfectly ripe melon and desserts with tropical fruit, or can be drunk as an aperitif. When served at 50°F (10°C), it is the perfect partner for *foie gras* and blue cheese.

Banyuls wines are bright terra-cotta in color, with aromas of toast and plums. Some are bottled at a young age, without oxidation, and are known as Rimage. White Banyuls, rarer and less well known, is a brilliant, light yellow in color with floral and fruit aromas. Note that the best ones are known as Banyuls Doré (golden) or Ambré (amber). Banyuls Grand Cru is only produced in exceptional years and has its own appellation. It is made from a minimum of 75 percent Grenache Noir and is an exceptional wine, with a terra-cotta color and complex, lingering aromas of spices, dried fruit, and

preserves. Rimage is a better accompaniment to melon than the port traditionally drunk by the French, and it also goes well with spicy foods and blue cheeses. This is also a perfect dessert wine, ideal with berry desserts. Furthermore, it is one of the few wines that can stand up to chocolate, making it a perfect companion to mousses, soufflés, and tarts with a high cocoa content. Banyuls Grand Cru and old Banyuls are excellent with honey-glazed duck, jugged hare, and crawfish, as well as with pheasant, game stews, crème caramel, and other creamy desserts.

Maury wines are produced from at least 75 percent Grenache Noir, and are aged in the traditional method in an oxidized environment. They develop mahogany tones and an aroma that hints at cocoa, and they have a surprising bouquet of blackberry jelly, fudge, pear, and spices. There are also some non-oxidized versions, known as Récolte and Vendange, that are bottled early. White Maury is a distinctive wine that can easily be drunk on its own, the perfect accompaniment to conversation far into the night, but it also goes well with the same foods as Banyuls, as well as sautéed *foie gras*.

DRY WINES

The wines of Collioure come in three colors. The reds are fleshy, powerful, and concentrated and go very well with smoked ham, paella, and the classic dishes of the area, such as rabbit with thyme, lamb with rosemary, ratatouille, Provençal stew, and escargots. When aged, they are the ideal wine for partnering classic cheeses from the Massif Central, such as Tomme, Laguiole, and Saler. The same grape varieties are used for rosé wines but with the addition of Grenache Gris. They are fruity, luxuriant, and warm, and are best drunk in the year after harvesting. Served chilled, they are perfect wines to accompany barbecues and also make good summer aperitifs. White Coullioure is a new appellation, created in July 2003, and is made predominantly of Grenache Blanc and Gris. The Grenache Gris is a very robust grape that produces structured wines with aromas of dried fruits. Grenache Blanc offers refined aniseed notes. Apart from these two main grape varieties, five others are permitted. Tourbat, or Malvoisie, has just the right degree of acidity and when young contains hints of ripe apple, developing cooked fruit and honey aromas as it ages. Macabeu gives floral and fruity aromas, which develop honeyed notes. Marsanne contributes smoothness to the wines, while Roussanne is full-bodied and complex, developing aromatic qualities in the cask. Finally, Vermentino provides freshness, aroma, richness, and balance. Grenache Blanc is perfect with all southern French fish dishes.

Côtes-du-Roussillon is made in red, white, and rosé. The red predominates, accounting for 80 percent of total production, while rosés represent 13 percent and white wines 7 percent. White Côtes-du-Roussillon wines are light, fine, fresh, floral, and fruity. The rosés are very fruity and quite full-bodied. The reds have berry aromas with spicy undertones. They are light and very approachable, but should be drunk young. Côtes-du-Roussillon Villages is a red wine only, and has more body than its Côtes-du-Roussillon counterparts. Depending on the *cuvée*, the aromas are more complex, often enhanced by aging in oak barrels. The varieties used are the same as for Côtes-du-Roussillon, but the wine is subject to additional quality constraints. Four *communes* are allowed to attach their names to that of the appellation, since their wine type is closely linked to the type of soil on which the grapes are grown. Thus, the wines of Lesquerde are light with mineral notes, and hints of violets and spices. Red Côtes-du-Roussillon and Côtes-du-Roussillon Villages can be drunk with the same sorts of foods, such as cured meats, red and white meat, and cow's milk cheeses. Côtes-du-Roussillon reds, however, also go well with mixed salads or in wine sauce, while the Villages appellation is a good accompaniment to ragout. The rosés are supple, fruity, and vigorous. They have a deep color, and develop aromas of cherry, plum, and licorice. They are the perfect accompaniment to fish soups and mixed salads.

ITINERARY

The Banyuls *terroir* is the most southerly in mainland France, and the landscape is reminiscent of that of the Douro valley in Portugal. Appellation Banyuls and Banyuls Grand Cru vines cover the hillsides above four ports of the Côte Vermeille—Cerbère, Banyuls, Port-Vendres, and Collioure. The plots of vines are very small, so that growers are unable to make a living just from the fruits of their vineyards. They thus have other occupations such as fishing, working their vineyards as if they were gardens. This partly explains why 75 percent of Roussillon grape growers do not vinify their own grapes and have to join cooperatives.

THE RIVER AGLY MEANDERS THROUGH SOME OF THE MOST ELEGANT PROPERTIES IN ROUSSILLON (FACING PAGE). THE SENSUAL MORNING MISTS THAT COAT THE RED GRAPE SKINS HAVE GIVEN THIS MAS BAUX WINE (RIGHT) ITS UNUSUAL LABEL AND NAME: ROUGE À LÈVRES (LIPSTICK). THE VILLAGE OF COLLIOURE (FOLLOWING DOUBLE PAGE), WHICH ONCE SERVED AS AN ARTISTS' COLONY FOR THE FAUVES, LENT ITS NAME IN JULY 2003 TO A NEW APPELLATION PRODUCING ALL THREE COLORS OF WINE.

THE CHÂTEAU DE JAU, NORTHEAST OF
PERPIGNAN (ABOVE), ALSO SERVES AS A GALLERY
FOR EXHIBITIONS OF CONTEMPORARY ART.
THE LABEL (FACING PAGE), DESIGNED BY THE ARTIST
BEN, IS IN THE SAME VEIN AS THE JAJA DE JAU,
A SIMPLE YET VERY DRINKABLE BISTRO WINE.

Banyuls-sur-Mer, where the Albères mountains plunge into the sea, is a sight for sore eyes. The rocky seashore is washed with the lapis-lazuli blue of the Mediterranean, and to the west the hills are blanketed with vine-covered terraces, supported by nearly four thousand miles (six thousand kilometers) of low shale walls known as *les peus de gall* (chicken's feet). This system of irrigation ditches, channeling the running water in such a way as to prevent erosion, was invented in the Middle Ages. Resembling stone sculptures, they have made an indelible mark on the countryside. The terraces are so fragile and inaccessible that the grapes have to be picked by hand, and it takes nine days just to pick two and a half acres (one hectare). It is laborious work but it doesn't end with the harvest. In winter, the earth and stones dislodged from the slopes by the rains have to be collected in wicker baskets and replaced. The low walls run alongside *casots*, country cottages with stone walls and red tiled roofs, adding to the charm of the unique *terroir*.

The people of Banyuls have two main occupations: seaside tourism and vine-growing. When the weather begins to turn, the summer visitors desert the beaches and head off in search of the wines at the Domaine de La Rectorie. In a brick-lined, underground air-raid shelter, dug out during World War II, drinkers sit at a large table resting on wine barrels, while Monsieur Parcé lectures on the subject of the ancient Banyuls, talking, for example, about the wine known as L'Oublié, produced thanks to the discovery of a forgotten barrel that had been left behind from several years earlier. This father of nine is indifferent to the vagaries of fashion and rejects the idea of being the creator of his wines. As far as he is concerned, they are part of history. He will tell you that the Grenache variety is very demanding and will not tolerate mediocrity or pretence. The grape demands honest and humble wine growers. It is difficult and austere, but can be compliant and tender, as well as strong and powerful. It is tenacious and faithful—just like Mediterranean women, he claims. In very hot years, it is the only grape that will withstand harsh treatment. It is not a varietal wine, possessing the modesty of greatness. To understand more about how it is cultivated, you should visit the Cellier des Templiers, which controls half of the production of this wine. Before visiting this immense and imposing winery, take a look at the museum which is very informative and illustrates the process of making these wines. The museum tour ends in the large tasting room, where the well-informed ask to taste white Collioure, Madeloc, the rosé Collioure, the Cuvée de la Salette and, red wines of the Domaine du Roumani, Château des Abelles, and Abbaye de Valbonne—the finest that this union of producers has to offer.

The walk to Port-Vendres on the Route des Crêtes, the D86, should not be missed. There are panoramic views all along this road, which goes from Cap Béar to Cap d'Agde, from the Côte Vermeille to the Albères mountains. Port-Vendres is the only deep bay in Languedoc-Roussillon and has a pier lined with bar-restaurants. This is a good place to try out some recently discovered wines, along with a few anchovies and other grilled fish. It is a good idea to join the people

Le jaja
de jau

Ben

The terrain in Banyuls (facing page) is steep and inaccessible, but winemakers have performed the Herculean task of leveling and terracing the soil. The end product is France's finest vin doux naturel, a superb accompaniment to any chocolate dessert. From the renowned Mas Amiel to the Muscat d'Alexandrie and Maury, the firm of Mas Amiel offers a wide range of magnificent organic wines with bold labels (right).

of Banyuls on the third weekend in October for the harvest festival held on the black pebble beach. The grapes arrive symbolically from the sea on decorated Catalan rowboats amid enthusiastic celebrations.

The N114 will take you all the way to Clos des Paulilles. This estate has 222 acres (90 hectares), forming the largest vineyard of Banyuls and Collioure wines. It borders one of the most beautiful bays in the region. In the evening, between Ascension weekend (mid-May) and September, the Dauré family offers a wine-tasting of ten of their estate's wines, along with a wonderful meal on the terrace of their farmhouse hotel, beneath the branches of a three-hundred-year-old mulberry tree. The estate's top wine is the delicious rosé. It is full-bodied with plenty of character and freshness, and tastes like a red wine. It goes wonderfully with Mediterranean shrimp, sea bass, sea bream, and all the other Mediterranean fish, and is perfect with garlicky, spicy dishes.

The Château de Valmy is also on the N114, near the Argelès exit. The château welcomes visitors. A rose bush is planted at the end of each row of vines, so that more than three thousand roses are planted in this way throughout the vineyard, which would not look out of place in the Médoc. The four-story mansion, a mass of curves is designed in an architectural style that is more Nordic than Mediterranean, which is hardly surprising since the architect was Danish. It has just undergone extensive refurbishment and is now open to the public as a guest house. There is a profusion of stained-glass windows, together with parquet and tiled flooring, all dating from 1900, and the five bedrooms have splendid views of the vineyard and the coast. The wine-tasting cellar is ultramodern and its huge glazed doors open into the high-tech stainless steel *chais*. This new estate produces four dry wines and a dessert wine, all great value for money.

The Domaine du Mas Baux is situated between Perpignan and Canet-en-Roussillon and has a fifty-acre (twenty-hectare) vineyard, of which thirty acres (twelve hectares) abut *garrigue*. This eighteenth-century, Catalan country house has been sensitively restored and has a cellar whose walls date from the sixteenth century. The tasting room would not look out of place between the covers of an interior design magazine. Serge and Marie-Pierre Baux, keen to invest in a winemaking venture, discovered this estate in the spring of 1997. They were captivated by the beauty of the setting and it was love at first sight, despite the dilapidated state of the buildings and the fact that the vines were in danger of being engulfed by the *garrigue* and overrun by ivy. They kept what deserved to be retained, namely the old Grenache Noir vines, and Serge set about replanting the rest of the vine stock, using his favorite grapes, which included Syrah, Mourvèdre, and Cabernet Sauvignon. The estate is fortunate enough to have superb views of the Pyrenees, Mont Canigou, and Corbières. It is well aired by breezes, very sunny, and just two and a half miles from the Mediterranean. Serge Baux readily admits that the secret of making great wines can be summed up in three words—time, time, and more time. Take your time, be patient, and always pick the right moment. Soleil Rouge (Red Sun), Rouge Gorge (Robin Redbreast), Rouge à Lèvres (Lipstick), and Beau Blond (Handsome Blond) are the names given to the wines produced here under the appellation Vin de Pays des Côtes Catalanes. Marie-Pierre, as president of the Festival de Perpignan, wanted to give these wines simple, sophisticated, and original labels, and indeed the bottles would enhance the most elegant of dinner tables. The ideal serving temperature of the wines is displayed in the form of a thermometer on the label. The Rouge à Levres, a *rosé de pays* made in the Côtes Catalanes, is an amazing wine—robust and smooth, but also highly feminine. It has floral and berry aromas, combined with gingerbread undertone.

Passing through the ancient city of Perpignan, you reach the village of Rivesaltes, famous for its *vins doux naturels*. Some good examples can be tasted at the Domaine de Rombeau or Domaine Cazes. Then visit the Château de Jau, located beside the river Agly, just outside

the small town of Case-de-Pène. You will find it by walking along a little road that winds through the Mediterranean landscape, where olive trees, cypresses, and vines grow side by side, serenaded by the noisy chorus of the cicadas. The ocher colors of the façades of the houses and the surrounding vegetation give the whole area a Tuscan air. What makes Jau so special is that its former silkworm breeding building now houses a modern art center and there is a summer restaurant where you can eat while drinking as much wine as you want, including the famous Jaja de Jau, a *vin de pays* of the Côtes Catalanes that can be drunk throughout the meal, without having to worry about what food you are eating. The superb label was designed by the artist Ben. Eight wines are produced on the estate, including a Côtes-du-Roussillon Villages characterized by its aromas of *garrigue*, spices, and berries. It is perfect with monkfish cooked in red wine, grilled meats, or slow cooked dishes, and it is the star wine of the estate. Côtes-du-Roussillon Villages Talon Rouge, on the other hand, is a fruity, silky, full-bodied, mellow wine with a deep nose containing overripe black berries, violet, and pear. It is honest, well balanced, and powerful.

Although the D117 will bring you directly to Mas Amiel, it is worth taking the dirt road just at the exit from the château that winds among the vines, so that you can take a small detour to the Château de Saint-Roc, also located by the river. The history of this estate dates back to 1816, when the bishop of Perpignan met Raymond Etienne Amiel, a civil engineer, at the gambling table. The bishop bet his estate, Quéribus, which is dominated by the octagonal keep of the old Cathar castle. He lost and that is how it came into the possession of the engineer. In October 1999, Olivier Decelle, chairman of the Picard frozen foods company, bought the Mas Amiel. From the first year of production, he decided to handle each plot of vines separately, so five teams share the running of the vineyard and manage the 370 acres (150 hectares) as if they were five estates of seventy-four acres (thirty hectares) each. They believe that, like all other plants, vines depend on their environment, and that the roots, fruits, and the flowers are influenced by the solar and lunar rhythms. As a result, they use the biodynamic method of cultivation. The Cuvée Charles Dupuy is vinified in the Portuguese manner, the grapes being pressed by foot. Its other original feature stems from the fact that it is aged for eighteen months in new barrels, giving it flavors of plum, caramel, spices, and pear. The wines should be served in a chilled glass and are the perfect accompaniment to foie gras and Roquefort, as well as chocolate desserts.

The Domaine de Caladroy lies between the Agly and Têt valleys at the foot of the Força Réal. Perched at an altitude of just over 1,000 feet (325 meters) above the Bélesta *commune*, it is the largest single spread in the *département*. This vast ocean of vines belongs to Michel Mezerette, owner of a large international transportation company. From the shady terrace, the view stretches out across the Roussillon plain toward Mont Canigou. The showcase of the estate is the cellar, built in the remains of a twelfth-century chapel, the shape of the elegant arches being emphasized by subtle plays of the light. In contrast to the traditional architecture, the vineyard has undergone a revolution. It has been completely redeveloped and replanted in order to produce four categories of wine: classic dry rosés and whites, the latter made from Chardonnay; natural dessert wines (Muscat de Rivesaltes, and Rivesaltes Ambré and Tuilé); and traditional wines (Schistes and Grenats). There are also special *cuvées*, such as Julianne, Cuvée Saint-Michel, and Cour Carrée. The latter is acclaimed for its dark red color, and red-and-black berry nose, mixed with toast and balsamic notes. In the mouth, the tannins are perfectly blended. The wine goes wonderfully with cheeses. Lovers of French apple pie (*tarte tatin*) and chocolate desserts, will find that Rivesaltes Ambré is the perfect accompaniment. This is a real feast of wines.

SOUTHERN
CÔTES-DU-RHÔNE

IN THE LUBÉRON, A REGION PERMEATED WITH A SENSE OF EASY LIVING,
TIGHTLY PACKED ROWS OF VINES LINE THE ROADS, AS HERE
IN THE VILLAGE OF MÉNERBES. THE WINES PRODUCED HERE
ARE LUMINOUS, FULL-BODIED, AND DEEP.

GRAPE VARIETIES
Grenache
Cinsault
Syrah
Mourvèdre
Muscardin
Clairette
Marsanne
Roussanne
Bourboulenc
Grenache blanc
Carignan

THE SOUTHERN RHÔNE VALLEY:
FROM THE MOST PRESTIGIOUS WINES
TO VACATION TIPPLE

This is a land of forgotten rural hamlets and picturesque villages crowned with a bell tower, of narrow, cobbled streets and squares shaded by massive plane trees, of roofs the color of toast and intensely blue skies, a land that breathes history from the tiniest tiny crack in an old wall. Wild and little known, this is a landscape of hills, rock, orchards, and vines, dominated by the rugged Dentelles de Montmirail.

This is a part of Provence that is hidden, wild, and steeped in tradition, an arid windswept landscape dotted with vineyards, lavender, olive trees, and truffle oaks. It is the land of the Mediterranean undergrowth, the *garrigue*. This Provence is influenced by the Rhône and its abundant pebbles, which were carried along by the current and have been ennobled by the exploits of winemakers. Although most local producers follow traditional practices, a new generation are enthusiastically embracing modern techniques. Their boldness has sometimes led to significant improvements in quality.

The Rhône valley is the second biggest wine district in France in terms of area and production, and is divided into two distinct parts, the northern Rhône valley (from south of Lyon to Valence) and the southern Rhône valley (from south of Montélimar to Avignon). The papal city of Avignon may be the capital of the Côtes-du-Rhône, but the southern vineyard covers a string of villages that have their own distinct personality.

Not surprisingly, it can be difficult to get to grips with this vast wine-producing area, whose prestigious appellations are dispersed across several regions. The southern part of the area can claim seven out of a total of thirteen wine-growing districts. They are Châteauneuf-du-Pape, Gigondas, Vacqueyras, Lirac, and Tavel, together with the *vins doux naturels* of Beaumes-de-Venise and Rasteau.

Although Côtes-du-Rhône Villages covers ninety-five communes, only sixteen of them can be named on the label. In the Vaucluse *département*, they are Beaumes-de-Venise, Cairanne, Rasteau, Roaix, Sablet, Séguret, Valréas, and Visan; in the Drôme *département*, Rochegude, Saint-Maurice, Saint-Pantaléon les Vignes, and Vinsobres; and in the Gard *département*, Chusclan, Laudun, and Saint-Gervais.

In all these appellations, in addition to the reds which make up the majority of wines produced, there are some great white wines, notably in Châteauneuf-du-Pape, and there are some lovely rosés everywhere. As for the *vins doux naturels*, such as the famous Beaumes-de-Venise, they tend to age rather better than people do.

The wines of the southern Côtes-du-Rhône come in all three colors and have very diverse personalities. But whether they be light and fruity, coarse and powerful, mild and sweet, or aromatic and sunny, all are the product of the divine trilogy of sun, wind, and grape varieties.

MADE FROM MUSCAT GRAPES, BEAUMES DE VENISE IS THE MOST FAMOUS DESSERT WINE IN FRANCE.
IT IS PALE GOLD IN HUE, AND HAS AN INTENSE NOSE OF ORANGE BLOSSOM AND A FULL, SWEET, VELVETY ATTACK.

CHÂTEAUNEUF-DU-PAPE:
THE FINEST WINE OF THE SOUTHERN RHÔNE VALLEY

This is a wine of long, silent contemplation and poetic paeans of praise. The embossed motif of the crossed keys of St. Peter against the papal crown that decorates bottles of Châteauneuf-du-Pape proves how divine this wine is.

This varied appellation, the most prestigious of the southern Rhône valley, is located between Orange and Avignon, at the foot of Mont Ventoux. It takes in the *communes* of Châteauneuf-du-Pape, Courthézon, Orange, Bédarrides, and Sorgues, covering an area of around 7,900 acres (3,200 hectares). In this landscape of low hills, the vineyards are carpeted with an expanse of smooth, rounded pebbles. The climate is Mediterranean, with more than two hundred days of sun a year. As for the mistral, the bitter north wind of the Midi, it actually has a beneficial influence on the vines. The rainfall enables the soil to build up important reserves of water, helping the vines to combat the hot, dry summers, while the pebbles act as a sort of thermostat, storing the heat of the day and gradually releasing it at night, thus helping the grapes to mature. During the Quaternary glaciation period, the waters of the Rhône swept these stones down from the Alps to the area now occupied by the highest vine-covered terraces. The combined action of the retreating sea and erosion caused by the river sculpted a relief of natural terraces and slopes right down to the present-day course of the Rhône. Of the vine stocks, 70 percent are Grenache, with Syrah coming a distant second at 11 percent and Mourvèdre trailing third at 7 percent. The vines are fairly mature (on average thirty-six years old), but it is not unusual to find plots planted with stock that is a hundred years old, such as the vines of the Château de La Nerthe or those grown on the Cabrières plateau.

Châteauneuf-du-Pape is distinctive in a number of ways. First of all, it has one of the lowest yields of any of the French appellation wines, producing only 374 gallons to the acre (thirty-five hectoliters to the hectare). Secondly, it has a minimum specified natural alcoholic strength of 12.5 percent, the highest in France. Lastly, the appellation permits thirteen different vine varieties, a record for French wines. Eight of them are red grapes: Grenache Noir and Cinsaut for warmth and mellowness; Syrah, Mourvèdre, Muscardin, and Vaccarèse for a solid foundation, consistency, and color; and Counoise and Terret for good vinosity, freshness, and bouquet. The five whites are Clairette and Bourboulenc, providing finesse and luminosity, Grenache Blanc and Roussane, adding elegance and complexity, and two lesser-known varieties, Picardan and Picpoul.

Although the white wines only represent 6 percent of total production, they are so successful that prices have shot up in recent years. They are very harmonious and surprisingly fresh and elegant, with a interestingly complex aromas. When young, up to three years old, they make wonderful companions to fish, shellfish, and white meats. When over five years of age, they develop delicious fragrances of honey, hazelnut, and toast. Surprisingly, they enhance the flavor of foie gras and combine very well with wild mushrooms such as chanterelles and ceps, as well as goat's cheese and soft cheeses with a floury rind. The combination with truffles is astonishing, the latter bringing out all the finesse of the wine. They should be served at about 54°F (12°C); below 50°F (10°C), they lose some of their aroma. The reputation of the reds is well established, of course, and they are particularly suited for laying down. Although they are deliciously fruity when young, they need patience, as they are magnificently voluptuous when aged—providing they are served at between 61°F (16°C) and 64°F (18°C). With their intense, deep bouquet and rich, spicy flavor, they are best partnered with strong-flavored game, red meat, broiled or barbecued lamb, and cheese.

A LITTLE HISTORY

The story of the papal vineyard, which has been classified as one of the *grands crus* of the Rhône valley, is linked to that of the

Château La Nerthe is reminiscent of some of the grander properties in the Médoc.
Its handsome façade dominates the road leading to the village of Châteauneuf-du-Pape.

river. The old name for Châteauneuf, Castro Novo, appears for the first time in a deed of gift ratified in 1094. In 1157, Geoffroy, bishop of Avignon, who remained faithful to the Roman custom of planting vines, already owned a vineyard at Châteauneuf. In the thirteenth century, this prosperous village had as many as a thousand inhabitants and owned 741 acres (300 hectares) of vineyards. In 1308, the first pope to have his seat in Avignon, Clement V, extended the vineyard even further. Pope John XXII made an even greater contribution to the reputation of this wine by exporting it to the Vatican and then bequeathing it the first denomination in its history, Vin du Pape ("The Pope's Wine"), the name by which it was known until it became Châteauneuf-du-Pape. From 1500 onward, this nectar acquired such fame that in his *Histoire de la Provence,* the great Nostradamus mentioned in flattering terms "Châteauneuf commonly known as de Pape, a place that produces excellent wines, several vessels of which are sent to Rome." Although it is not known which varieties were planted in the region prior to the eighteenth century, Châteauneuf was reputed to be a "warm yet delicate wine which ought to be drunk after four years." A century later, the Provençal winemaker and writer Anselme Mathieu had the brilliant idea of selling some of the bottles of wine he produced, adorned with a handsome label bearing the title Vin di Felibre (in Provençal), together with the words "The wine of Châteauneuf gives courage and song and love and joy." Other French writers who sang its praises include Alphonse de Lamartine, Alexandre Dumas, and Alphonse Daudet, the latter becoming gloriously drunk on this imperial and pontifical wine, thanks to his friend and fellow author, the poet Frédéric Mistral.

In the early 1870s, the vineyards were devastated by phylloxera and reconstruction proved a costly business. In 1893, at the request of the mayor, Joseph Ducos, who was also the owner of Château de La Nerthe, the village adopted the name of Châteauneuf-du-Pape. The most active of the producers was Baron Le Roy de Boiseaumarié (1890–1967), who was both a winemaker and lawyer. It was he who, with the help of his peers, fixed the rules that eventually served as a prototype for the famous Appellation d'Origine Contrôlée system that now governs all locally made specialty food and drink in France.

ITINERARY

The D17 that links Avignon and Châteauneuf-du-Pape is lined with magnificent châteaux that are emblematic of the importance of Châteauneuf-du-Pape in the world of wine. The first of these, La Nerthe, is partially concealed by a forest of plane and hackberry trees. An avenue of cypresses more than a century old leads the visitor to the south façade, whose magnificent eighteenth-century frontage is shaded by live oaks and Aleppo pines. The château has been used as a location for many films, and would look at home in the

BELOW: ONE OF THE THIRTEEN VARIETIES GROWN IN THIS AOC. CHÂTEAU LA NERTHE PRODUCES SOME OF THE FINEST WINES OF THE CHÂTEAUNEUF-DU-PAPE APPELLATION. ITS CELLARS (FACING PAGE) CONCEAL AGELESS OAK CASKS AND ENDLESS ROWS OF BARRELS IN WHICH THE WINES ARE ALLOWED TO MATURE SERENELY.

Médoc. A handsome tasting room has been created in the former orangery. The renaissance of La Nerthe is due to the excellent management of Alain Dugas. By creating wines in the modern style without sacrificing any of the typical features of Châteauneuf, this shrewd winemaker has restored the luster to a domain considered one of the finest architectural gems of the region. A visit to the *chais*, believed to be the oldest in France, is a revelation. Five bottle-shaped vats holding 5,016 gallons (190 hectoliters) each were carved into the rock in 1560. Facing them, the racks on which bottles are stored for aging are labeled with the names of such Michelin-starred chefs as Alain Ducasse and Michel Bras, alongside those of anonymous multimillionaires resident in Monaco or the United States. The brick-lined tunnel containing the *barriques* is around fifty yards long and was built at the same time as the château. The last part is cut off by four-ton stone blocks taken from the Roman theater at Orange. There is another cellar a little further on, built in the nineteenth century and used as a bottle library, whose oldest vintages date from 1977, the older wines having naturally followed the last owners. At La Nerthe, before the phylloxera plague, as many white as red wines were made, as can be seen from the oldest archives of the appellation. Alain Dugas's philosophy is to ensure that the wines are balanced. Two hundred acres (eighty hectares) of grapes grown organically and twelve acres (five hectares) biodynamically make it possible to create the finest selections from the thirteen varieties of grape. The red Les Cadettes, which benefits from long maceration, is outstanding. Matured in vats for a year and bottled eighteen months after harvesting, it is luminous and deep in appearance with an intense, complex bouquet and a subtle texture in the mouth. The white Clos de Beauvenir, which bears the estate's former

name, is aged for eighteen months in oak and is a testament to the rigor and skill exercised here. The white wines of La Nerthe are ample and elegant, classic and distinguished, and are regarded as being among the finest of the appellation.

Next door to Château de La Nerthe is Château des Fines Roches, another example of the lavish architectural heritage of the region. This neo-medieval structure, covered in turrets, crenellations, and machicolations, looks more like a Scottish baronial hall devoted to whiskey distillation than a winemaking estate. In fact, this elaborate edifice was built in the early twentieth century principally to conceal the cellar. One can only admire the audacity and imagination needed to create such a distinctive building in the heart of this sun-kissed countryside, dotted with cypresses and popular with vacationers. After buying Château des Fines Roches in 1932, the manager of the Grandes Caves de Lyon decided to invest his family's future in it. The château was converted into a delightful hotel and restaurant, which the family leased out while retaining the cellar to make their wines. Gaëlle Barrot, one of his daughters, had just graduated in enology and was still in her twenties when she made her first vintage wine in 2000. Rounded, well structured, and elegant, it was a resounding success. Since then, the winemaking techniques have been further refined, and the wines, notable for their silky and aromatic bouquet, are regularly recommended by the foremost wine writers following tastings.

A few hundred yards away lies the avenue of cypresses belonging to the Château Fortia, which has one of the finest views of the village. This slightly dilapidated but charming country house still belongs to the family of Baron Le Roy de Boiseaumarié, who initiated the whole French concept of Appellations d'Origine Contrôlées in the 1930s. The wine was neglected for some time, but was revived thanks to the vigorous efforts of the owners, including Bruno Le Roy, the current president of the Fédération des Syndicats de

Producteurs and creator of the Cuvée du Baron, a fruity red of great finesse, the first vintage of which was produced in 2001. The Château de Beaucastel was bought in 1909 by an ancestor of the current owner, a scientist with a passion for wine. The château, which was used as a hunting lodge by Capitaine de Beaucastel in 1687, resembles a typical Provençal *mas*. The visionary predecessor of the present owner had a true understanding of the historic quality of the site and, in 1910, he planted ancient varieties that had almost disappeared, such as Mourvèdre and Counoise. In 1950, he converted the estate to organic cultivation, a revolutionary choice for the region in those days. Thanks to its historical commitment to high quality, Beaucastel can now claim to be one of the finest and most natural wines of the appellation. As well as 190 acres (77 hectares) of Châteauneuf-du-Pape—172 acres (70 hectares) of red and seventeen acres (seven hectares) of white—it has seventy-four acres (thirty hectares) of Côtes-du-Rhône. The latter is sold under the name Coudoulet de Beaucastel. Since the winemakers here are convinced that, in order to produce good wine, vines must be allowed to grow as naturally as possible, all the weeding is performed by hand, using a plow, and any sprays used on the vines are organic. Naturally, production is limited, but it expresses the quintessence of the *terroir*. The wines of Beaucastel are best drunk with food. The longstanding commitment to organic methods results in a dark red wine with a nose of berries, leather, truffles, and musk, and a flavor that is redolent of spices, pepper, and licorice. As for the white, based on Roussanne and Grenache Blanc, it is bottled after eight months of maturation. It is pale yellow in color, with aromas of honey, citrus, and acacia flowers. In the mouth it is syrupy, with a suggestion of honey and toast. Quite simply, these are some of the best wines of the appellation.

CÔTES-DU-RHÔNE VILLAGES:
GREAT WINES UNDER A MODEST APPELLATION

Between the Coteaux du Tricastin and an imaginary line drawn between Orange and Carpentras, several thousand acres of vineyards belonging to a number of different appellations carpet the slopes, terraces, and vast plains. The region encompasses the huge Côtes-du-Rhône appellation, which straddles the Rhône and covers around 100,000 acres (40,200 hectares), and the Côtes-du-Rhône Villages appellation, which is smaller but of higher quality. The Villages wines, whether red, white, or rosé, are subject to stricter regulations than those governing Côtes-du-Rhône wines. As a result, they are more concentrated and have greater finesse. The total area dedicated to the Villages appellation is 24,000 acres (9,500 hectares), around half of which is used to make wines bearing the name of a specific *commune*. Although the Côtes-du-Rhône Villages appellation encompasses ninety-five *communes* throughout the *départements* of the Drôme, Vaucluse, Gard, and Ardèche, only eight of the sixteen *communes* that are allowed to append their name to the appellation are in the Vaucluse. These are Beaumes-de-Venise, Cairanne, Rasteau, Roaix, Valréas, Visan, Sablet, and Séguret. In all these areas wine tourism is expanding rapidly.

The average yields are forty-five hectoliters per hectare (480 gallons per acre) for Côtes-du-Rhône Villages wines and forty-two hectoliters per hectare (449 gallons per acre) for Côtes-du-Rhône Villages wines from named *communes*. The alcohol content for these wines is 12 percent and 12.5 percent respectively.

For red wines, the appellation stipulates that half of the vine stock must be Grenache, and a lower percentage (but not less than 20 percent) must be Syrah and/or Mourvèdre. For rosé wines, Grenache is still the main variety, but the proportion of Syrah and/or Mourvèdre may be higher. For white wines, Grenache Blanc, Clairette, Marsanne, Roussane, Bourboulenc, and Viognier all share the limelight. The reds are full-bodied and combine well with game and all types of stuffed vegetable dishes. The white wines have subtle floral undertones and are the perfect accompaniment to hot or cold seafood, poultry cooked in a cream sauce, and cheeses such as blue cheese and fresh goat cheese. The rosés, with their fruity aromas, can be drunk with raw vegetables and mixed salads, as well as pizzas and couscous.

ITINERARY

Five miles north of Orange lies the Château Saint-Estève d'Uchaux. On arriving at the château, you cannot fail to be impressed by the elegant façade and the wooded hills of the Massif d'Uchaux that form a backdrop. The château's eighteenth-century vaulted wine cellar is magnificent, but it is the "Liszt en Provence" festival held here which has put the château in the spotlight. From its 150 acres (60 hectares) of Côtes-du-Rhône Villages vines, Saint Estève d'Uchaux produces white wines of wonderful quality with a lovely luminous color. The three white *cuvées*, made principally from Viognier using traditional methods, are all stunning, but the best is Thérèse, named after the lady of the manor. This is a wine of rare opulence and purity that has all the qualities of a *grand cru*, and it even ages well. It makes a delightful aperitif or after-dinner drink. As for the red wines, the Tradition, with its aromas of berries and spices, is very popular, but it is the Grande Réserve, made predominantly with Syrah grapes from the best plots and aged in oak casks, which delights connoisseurs. Saint-Estève is run by a charming and hospitable couple, whose love of music dovetails perfectly with their love of wine.

On leaving the château, turn left and continue along the road to the neighboring Domaine de la Renjarde. It is difficult to resist

VAL JOANIS ROSÉ, THE IDEAL APERITIF, IS A WELL-BALANCED WINE THAT IS BURSTING WITH BERRY FLAVORS.
IT GOES DELIGHTFULLY WITH THE REGIONAL CUISINES OF THE SOUTH OF FRANCE AND EVEN WITH MOROCCAN FOOD.

the charm of this winery, which seems to epitomize the South of France. Wine tasting is held in a building designed to look like a typical Provençal house, the vibrant hues offsetting the raspberry-colored walls. Here you can taste the wine as you would among friends, lounging in deep tobacco-colored sofas arranged around the hearth, or at the large wood-and-wrought-iron table in the dining room. To clear your head after the tasting, you can take a pleasant stroll around the outside of the house, where you can view the new plots that have been acquired on the south-facing slopes and catch a glimpse of the spectacular pool to the rear. The pool was discovered while the ground was being levelled. It dates from the Roman era and has a single column standing in the center. The owner of the estate, Alain Degas, is well known to all wine enthusiasts, since he has been entrusted with one of the finest of the Châteauneuf-du-Pape wines, Château de La Nerthe. He chose to live here at La Renjarde, however, where he exercises the same attention to detail and expertise. The resulting red wines are excellent value for money, displaying great complexity and finesse.

Having made his fortune drilling for oil, Walter McKinley, then aged sixty, sold his business and his three restaurants in order to realize his dream of owning a winery. In 1994 he founded Domaine de Mourchon, situated above the picturesque village of Séguret at an altitude of about one thousand feet (three hundred meters) amid the spectacular scenery of the Dentelles de Montmirail. The Scots may have a reputation for being frugal, but there is plenty of evidence here that no expense was spared. The villa was constructed in the Tuscan style, on the ruins of a former charcoal-burner's house; it has a terrace surrounded by colonnades and plantings of cypress trees. The old stones have been cleverly arranged in an uneven fashion to give the carefully studied impression of age. There is also a patio, a huge swimming pool, an entrance porch, and an impressive fountain in front of the house. Before entering the wine-tasting cellar, take the steep path up the hill to the side of the house, from where you have a wonderful view over the whole property. McKinley is as demanding in his winemaking as he is in his lifestyle and nothing is left to chance. Since his first effort in 1999, his wines have become increasingly refined, garnering praise from many quarters. Particularly fine is his deep purple Grande Réserve, with its nose rich in notes of spices and licorice, combined with berry preserves. In the mouth it is full-bodied, rounded, and rich, with balanced tannins. In short, this is a wine that matches the lofty ambitions of the owner.

WITH ITS STONE HOUSES AND COBBLED LANES, SÉGURET IS QUINTESSENTIALLY PROVENÇAL AND HAS BEEN CLASSED AS ONE OF THE MOST PICTURESQUE VILLAGES IN FRANCE. LOCATED AT THE NORTHERN END OF THE DENTELLES DE MONTMIRAIL AND WEST OF MONT VENTOUX, IN THE HEART OF THE CÔTES-DU-RHÔNE VILLAGES APPELLATION, ITS WINES HAVE A SILKY TEXTURE WITH BERRY AROMAS.

GIGONDAS: POWERFUL AND GENEROUS REDS

As if afraid of falling, the village of Gigondas clings to the foothills of the peaks known as the Dentelles de Montmirail. Women will have to leave their high heels at home if they want to explore this little hillside fortress, but they will be rewarded with a stunning view. Here the jagged limestone ridges of the Dentelles tower above orchards, hills, and vines, offering a landscape of stunning contrasts. The Roman name of the village comes from the Latin *Jucunditas,* meaning joy and light-heartedness, proving to what extent Gigondas has always been a good place to live. In fact, that is exactly how you feel when you contemplate the view from the château next to the church as it stretches away toward the distant Cévennes. This village, with its many fountains, front doors patinated with age, and steep streets, has lent its name to one of the most illustrious red wine appellations of the Rhône valley.

Roman centurions who owned villas in the area were the first to plant vines, and yet until the middle of the twentieth century the landscape was dominated by olive trees, grape-growing being a secondary activity. Nowadays, the villagers are engaged entirely in growing grapes and making wines, and the vineyard covers an area of 3,038 acres (1,230 hectares) scattered throughout the *commune.*

Gigondas wine was once used to "fortify" Burgundy, but it is now considered the best red wine in the southern Côtes-du-Rhône, after Châteauneuf-du-Pape. In fact, the red and rosé wines received the supreme recognition of being awarded an appellation in 1971. The wine is also considered to be the most powerful in the Rhône valley. It is made mainly from Grenache, which can be used for as much as 80 percent of the blend, the rest being made up of Syrah and Mourvèdre.

The vineyards of Gigondas can vary in altitude between 800 feet (250 meters) and 1,700 feet (500 meters) on the northern slope of the Dentelles range, which explains why there is a difference of two weeks in ripening between the highest and lowest plots of the appellation, creating a good ratio for making balanced the wines.

This dark, intense, alluring wine is very distinctive. Made for laying down, it is tannic and full-bodied. Although it can be heavy and coarse when poorly made, in expert hands it has a nose of berries and kirsch and sometimes of ripe fruits and jam. It is slightly peppery when young, taking on wilder nuances of undergrowth as it ages. It goes well with game, spicy food, and strongly flavored cheese. Although 90 percent of Gigondas wines are red, the rosés are heady and generous, and have characteristic aromas of almonds, berries, and spices. The only imperative with these liquid delights is that they must be drunk in the year in which they were made.

ITINERARY

The Château de Saint-Cosme, which has been owned by the same family since 1490, lies at the bottom of the village and is actually a large country house. It is surrounded by a large and beautiful park, overlooked by a little Romanesque chapel from which it gets it name. The entrance to the fifteenth-century wine cellars is unremarkable, and once inside it is something of a surprise to discover four Gallo-Roman basins cut into the rock. Negotiating your way around the cases of wine, you will find a collection of winemaking equipment of great archeological interest, including glass bottles dating from Roman times. At Saint-Cosme, the vines surrounding the château have been planted on a mosaic of plots, a result of the geological chaos of the Dentelles, whose presence creates a cool, late-ripening microclimate in this part of the appellation. The interaction between geology and microclimate results in atypical Gigondas wines, which combine concentration, exuberance, and finesse.

CHÂTEAU RASPAIL IS ONE OF THE LEADING GIGONDAS ESTATES. ITS VIGOROUS, STRONG REDS ARE THE IDEAL COMPANION TO RED MEAT DISHES AND VEGETABLE GRATINS.

Operations are run by Louis Barruol, who took over from his father in 1997. His barrel-aged red has a ripe, fresh nose, with a subtle blend of spicy cherries, marc, and green and black pepper. In the mouth it is elegant and tasty, warm but not excessively so, with a slight sensation of residual sugar. Without doubt, Saint-Cosme is one of the stars of Gigondas.

Château Raspail is located to the east of the village, beside the road that leads to Sablet. Set in a carefully tended little park, it is perhaps the prettiest estate in the region. It was built in the Italian style in 1866 by Eugène Raspail, nephew of a famous French physician. With its façade reminiscent of the palazzos built around Lake Como, it has a refinement worthy of a distinguished aristocratic residence. It was by selling a Greek statue to the British Museum that Eugène had bought for next to nothing from a peasant in Vaison-la-Romaine that he could afford to build this little palace. In 1979, it was bought by the Meffre family, leading merchants in the region. The vineyard of 105 acres (42 hectares) is all of one piece and surrounds the château. Like the latter, it is impeccably maintained. Christian Meffre, who makes the only Gigondas that is sold by the Nicolas firm of wine merchants, has invested heavily to achieve optimum quality. In order to store the wines under the most favorable conditions, he covered the interior of his cement vats with epoxy resin. In addition to its classic Gigondas, this exemplary estate makes a more woody red called Vieilles Vignes, of which only five thousand bottles are produced. These strong but well-balanced wines, made from two-thirds Grenache and one third Syrah, should be left to mature for at least three years before drinking. In addition to the two reds, Christian Meffre has created an original Marc de Gigondas, which is only made from the best vintages. This brandy is made from what remains in the vat once the wine has been drawn off, distilled to 42 percent alcohol. Marc de Gigondas should be drunk like a cognac or an armagnac—that is to say, with a good cigar.

THE VILLAGE OF GIGONDAS (FACING PAGE) CLINGS PRECARIOUSLY TO THE STEEP SLOPES OF THE DENTELLES DE MONTMIRAIL, THE RED WINES OF ITS APPELLATION HAVING LEGENDARY POWER. STANDING AMONG THE VINES AT THE FOOT OF THE PICTURESQUE SÉGURET ESTATE, THE CABASSE ESTATE (BELOW) IS BOTH A HOTEL, A TRADITIONAL RESTAURANT, AND A WINE THAT DOES HONOR TO ITS TERROIR.

VACQUEYRAS:
WINEMAKERS FOR GENERATIONS

The N7 climbs steeply up to the village of Vacqueyras, centered around its picturesque Provençal bell tower. The vines keep a low profile on this spur of hills, preferring the southern slope, where they sweep across *garrigue* and mountain alike. Located in the Vaucluse *département*, in a region highly popular with tourists, barely a mile from its neighbor Gigondas, Vacqueyras has given its name to the only "Left Bank" Côtes-du-Rhône appellation producing wines in three colors. The vineyards, which extend to the foot of the Dentelles de Montmirail, encompass two *communes*: Vacqueyras and Sarrians. It covers an area of around 3,200 acres (1,300 hectares) and produces 97 percent reds, 1 percent whites, and 2 percent rosés. There are 185 wine growers in this appellation, but only fifty-five bottle their own wines and sell them from their properties. Ninety-five percent of the appellation is planted with reds, with Grenache Noir the most predominant, followed by Syrah, Cinsault, and Mourvèdre. For the rosés, winemakers resort to that old favorite, Grenache, which can account for up to 60 percent of the blend, together with Mourvèdre and Cinsault. As for the tiny, almost secretive production of whites, a minimum of 80 percent must be made up of the following six varieties: Clairette, Grenache Blanc, Bourboulenc, Roussanne, Marsanne, and Viognier.

The first documentation attesting to the existence of this vineyard dates from 1448 and takes the form of records of taxes collected by the provost of Orange on harvests of grapes and wine in Vacqueyras. In 1791, when the Comtat Venaissin (now the Vaucluse *département*) was restored to France, the existing vineyards—Châteauneuf, Gigondas, Sainte-Cécile, and Vacqueyras—were attached to the Côtes-du-Rhône. At the time, the village owned more than six thousand vines. After the decree that awarded an Appellation d'Origine Contrôlée to the Côtes-du-Rhône in 1937, Vacqueyras was one of the first villages to be recognized for the quality of its wines. In 1955, its wines were classified as Côtes-du-Rhône Vacqueyras, then Côtes-du-Rhône Villages Vacqueyras in 1990. The official wine of the Festival d'Avignon finally got its own separate appellation in 1995.

The *terroirs* here are less uniform than at Gigondas and the wines are lighter and more supple, less tannic and concentrated. The reds have a deep madder color, tinged with ruby in young wines and deepening to a pronounced garnet color with age. The have a bouquet of ripe fruits, black cherries, and hazelnut, with a hint of licorice and violet. In the mouth they are robust and sturdy, with good length. The most age-worthy examples, which may be kept for between seven and ten years, develop fragrances of licorice, undergrowth, pepper, and spices. With their delicious balance between fresh fruit and spices, the reds should be served at between 62°F and 64°F (17°C to 18°C), and are ideal partners for red meats and cheeses. The rosés are full and generous, with a flavor of strawberries and a fruity bouquet that combines well with Provençal dishes and exotic foods. Pale yellow with a floral nose, the whites are fresh, fruity, and rounded.

The appellation's Burgundy-style bottle bearing the coat of arms of the Syndicat des Vignerons de Vacqueyras has been modified recently. The color was changed from the yellow-green known as *feuille morte* to the dark brown of the *teinte antique*. The ring around the neck is now wider and the coat of arms set in deeper relief, with the keys engraved in the top part and the name Vacqueyras running across the lower part above the words "appellation contrôlée."

ITINERARY

It is impossible to miss Domaine La Fourmone, as it stands right beside the main road. Although you will not find an elegant château, stunning farmhouse, or stylishly renovated *mas* here, you

THE ATMOSPHERE IN VACQUEYRAS ON JULY 14, BASTILLE DAY, IS REMINISCENT OF THAT OF THE FAMOUS
MOULIN DE LA GALETTE IN MONTMARTRE. REVELERS ENJOY THEMSELVES HERE UNDER THE GREAT
PLANE TREES OF THE CENTRAL SQUARE, SAMPLING THEIR FAMOUS LOCAL WINES IN ALL THREE COLORS.

will certainly receive an enthusiastic welcome and ample evidence of this domaine's commitment to producing fine wine. Although the estate has made wine since the seventeenth century, vines were just part of the agricultural activity. The new buildings have been added to what was a simple dwelling, with the *chais* displacing the haylofts, sheepfolds, and silkworm breeding rooms of old. The motto of the estate is "Raço Racejo"—the race perpetuates itself, the tradition continues—and that is how this ninety-one acre (thirty-seven hectare) spread, run by two sisters, has acquired its reputation. Vacqueyras, Côtes-du-Rhône, and Gigondas wines are made here. The Cuvée Fleurantine is a Vacqueyras white made from a harmonious blend of Clairette and Grenache. Pale yellow with a green tinge, it has a bouquet of flowers and soft fruit, and a fresh flavor. The red Trésor du Poète, a blend of Grenache and Syrah, is a wine that has a nose of strawberry jam, licorice, and milk toffee—in short, all the delicious foods of childhood.

Château de Montmirail stands on the southern slopes of the Dentelles and is reached by a path bordered with trees. Some people venture here assuming it is the château of that name depicted in the French comedy *Les Visiteurs*. Sarah Bernhardt and Frédéric Mistral were among those who once came to take the waters at this famous spa. The brick-and-stone château was built in 1870, and with its sloping roofs and two gables it looks more like a curate's house in town than a Provençal dwelling. The family owned not only the hot springs, but also the entire Dentelles range; the father of the current owner acquired the land in 1965 and the château ten years later. The sixty-two acres (twenty-five hectares) of vines which adjoin the property and climb halfway up the slope of the mountain, which has wonderful trails for hikers, are actually classified under Gigondas. The forty-two acres (seventeen hectares) of Vacqueyras are dotted around the plateau, former scrubland where the sunshine is virtually

uninterrupted. Montmirail is one of three estates in the appellation run by women. All the château's Vacqueyras reds are made with combinations of Grenache and Syrah. The Cuvée des Deux Frères, made without oak, has strong red-fruit aromas and is rich and chewy in the mouth. The Cuvée des Saints Papes, the estate's top Vacqueyras red, spends eight months in oak barrels and is worth laying down for a year or two. The wines can be tasted not at the château, but rather in the childhood home of the owner's father, situated right in the center of the village.

THE DENTELLES DE MONTMIRAIL, ALSO KNOWN EVEN
MORE POETICALLY AS THE DENTELLES SARRASINES,
ARE A CHAIN OF SMALL MOUNTAINS IN THE NORTHERN
PART OF THE VAUCLUSE. THE TALLEST PEAK RISES
TO A HEIGHT OF 2,480 FEET (743 METERS) AND THE
SLOPES ARE SHARED BY THREE APPELLATIONS:
BEAUMES DE VENISE, VACQUEYRAS, AND GIGONDAS.

CÔTES-DU-VENTOUX: DELIGHTFUL LIGHT WINES

The vineyards of Côtes-du-Ventoux are located in the southern Rhône valley, a region of truck farms and historic towns that seems tailor-made for the good life. The appellation is in the shape of a huge arc, bordered to the northwest by the Gigondas, Vacqueyras, and Beaumes-de-Venise vineyards, and to the east by Avignon. It covers 19,266 acres (7,800 hectares) in the Vaucluse *département* and in part of the Comtat Venaissin. It is sheltered by the "Giant of Provence," the famous Mont Ventoux, with its legendary peak that is usually shrouded in mist. Life is truly a rural idyll here, in tune with the earth and the weather, revolving around the cherry, olive, truffle, almond, and—most importantly—the grape. Mont Ventoux itself is a ridge running from east to west that reaches a peak of 1,909 meters (about 6,263 feet). The vines are planted on the south-facing slope. The grapes from the 7,800 hectares (about 19,266 acres) are vinified by fifteen cooperatives and 120 individual cellars, producing 80 percent reds, 17 percent rosés, and 3 percent whites.

Although the grape varieties are similar to those of appellation wines from the southern Rhône valley, the presence of Mont Ventoux and its unique climate give them their own special characteristics. The grapes used for red and rosé wines are Grenache Noir, Syrah, Cinsaut, Mourvèdre, and Carignan, with lesser quantities of Picpoul Noir, and Counoise. The white wine varieties are Clairette, Bourboulenc, and Grenache Blanc, with smaller quantities of Ugni Blanc, Roussanne, Picpoul, and Pascal Blanc.

One of the most profitable of French appellations in terms of production, Côtes-du-Ventoux offers wines that are excellent value for money. The reds are bursting with berries and spicy aromas, with subtle truffle, pine, and *garrigue* flavors. The elegant rosés have floral notes of rosebud and broom flower combined with hints of cherry and raspberry. The whites are imbued with acacia and linden fragrances, mixed with elegant touches of pear, green apple, almond, and citrus.

Although winemaking in France can be dated back to the fifth century B.C., the discovery of a Roman wine-vessel workshop within this appellation has made it possible to date wine production in this region to 30 B.C. The development of viticulture and the production of high-quality wines in this region owe much to the presence of the Avignon popes. Between 1309 and 1414, the wines were often served to the popes and their guests in Avignon. But their fame was not limited to the papal court. In the nineteenth century, Louis-Philippe of France chose an old Grenache from Ventoux as the wine to be served at court. Côtes-du-Ventoux wines were designated Vin Delimité de Qualité Supérieure in 1953, acquiring full Appellation d'Origine Contrôlée status in July 1973. This young appellation is experiencing a substantial improvement in quality, thanks to the emergence of growers—some of whom have colorful personalities—committed to realizing the potential of the *terroir*.

ITINERARY

The Château d'Unang, at more than a thousand years old, is the oldest château in the Vaucluse, although in its current form it dates from between 1771 and 1784. This majestic residence, with its huge terrace that overlooks the grounds, is the most beautiful property in the region. For a long time open to the public, this château can sadly no longer be visited and is currently the very private domain of an Englishman. However, it is still possible to visit the wine cellar, where the estate's wines can be tasted; they are typical of the appellation.

Château Pesquié, one of the region's flagship wineries, is approached along a drive lined with thirty-four plane trees. From the terrace of the wine-tasting building there is a stunning view of the residence and the small village of Mormoiron. With its sun-drenched

DOMAINE DE FONDRÈCHE AND DOMAINE DE LA BASTIDONNE ARE AT THE FOREFRONT OF ESTATES IN THE CÔTES-DU-VENTOUX AND HAVE GARNERED CONSIDERABLE PRAISE FROM WINE WRITERS. THEIR WINES ARE ALSO POPULAR FOR BEING PARTICULARLY GOOD VALUE.

2003

~~INE~~ DE LA BASTIDONNE

~~S~~ DU VENTOUX

~~ON~~ CÔTES DU VENTOUX ~~CONTRÔLÉE~~

~~BOUTEILLE~~ ~~AU~~ DOMAINE

~~PRIÉTAIRES RÉCOLTANTS~~ ~~MARREAU~~

~~AVIGNON~~ 84220 VAUCLUSE - FRANCE

PRODUCT OF FRANCE

750 ml

DOMAINE DE
FONDRÈCHE

Côtes du Ventoux

Appellation Côtes du Ventoux Contrôlée

Cuvée NADAL

walls, cloth-covered tables, and frescoed bar, the building is an ideal setting for fine food and drink. Everything here seems to be designed to indulge the senses, inviting you to linger. You will certainly need to spend time here if you wish to explore both the history of the estate and the wide range of wines produced here. In 1985, Paul and Édith Chaudière, a physiotherapist and a speech therapist respectively from the Avignon region, gave up their careers and decided to return to their roots in winemaking. At the time, the number of independent winemakers working on the appellation's wines was very small. While studying at Suze-la-Rousse University for four years, the couple reorganized things, uprooting and then replanting their vineyard, introducing higher-quality varieties while making the most of the old vines. The vineyard now covers an area of 172 acres (70 hectares), of which about 90 percent is used for the Côtes-du-Ventoux appellation. In 1989, they decided to leave the cooperative in order to make wine in their own style. Paul's father was an agricultural engineer and professor of enology, and had taught his son a great deal about wine. Using his father's methods, Paul built new *chais* half-sunken in a former cherry orchard so that the grape harvest could be transferred by gravity. Les Terrasses, 60 percent Grenache and 40 percent Syrah, is made from vines thirty to sixty years old, and is partially aged in oak. Deep ruby/purple in color, it has a bouquet bursting with red fruits laced with spices and is a perfect accompaniment to stuffed baby vegetables or mushroom tart. The Quintessence, made from Grenache grapes from vines over fifty years old blended with Syrah, is aged for twelve months in new oak. Rich and unctuous, it is a good choice for drinking with roasts and soft cheese.

Surrounded by vines and an ornate garden, Château Talaud is a handsome eighteenth-century residence. It was bought in 1985 by a Dutch couple who had fallen in love with the place, and since then they have opened their doors to passing travelers. The façade is particularly impressive and has a balcony with a cast-iron balustrade that is one of the most beautiful examples of its kind in the Comtat Venaissin. Some of the windows overlook a poplar grove on a steep slope buffeted by the mistral, while others offer a great view of the thirty acres (twelve hectares) of vines. After breakfast has been served, the host slips into his role as the "gentleman farmer" and climbs on his tractor to go and inspect his Grenache and Syrah. Encouraged by the award of a bronze medal in 1999 for his first wine, he has gone on to create two *cuvées*, Cornelia and Antoine, named for his wife and son.

(FACING PAGE) DETAIL OF THE CHAPEL IN THE CHÂTEAU DE SUZE-LA-ROUSSE, REBUILT IN THE RENAISSANCE, THAT HAS BECOME THE UNIVERSITY OF WINE. THE CÔTES-DU-VENTOUX APPELLATION SPREADS OVER THE SOUTH FACE OF THE PEAK KNOWN AS THE GÉANT DE PROVENCE. THE EXUBERANT REDS HAVE A BOUQUET OF FRUIT AND SWEET SPICES AND THE WHITES ARE IMBUED WITH THE FRAGRANCES OF LIME AND ACACIA. THE ROSÉS ARE ROSEBUD PINK IN COLOR.

CÔTES-DU-LUBÉRON:
FASHIONABLE WINES FOR DRINKING ALL YEAR AROUND

A jumble of bright greens and blues, ancient villages spiraling around their church, the stridulation of grasshoppers at siesta time—here under the brilliant light of an eternal sun lies the very soul of wine. In this land of laidback living, with its hillsides covered in cherry trees and cypresses standing as erect as guards, nature is abundant and admirably preserved. The Lubéron has some of the finest places in France for lovers of natural beauty, fine things, and happiness.

The appellation is unusual in that it is part of a national park: the Parc National Régional du Lubéron. One of the first to be created in France, the park covers an area of 300,000 acres (120,000 hectares) east of Avignon and encompasses two other appellations, the Côtes-du-Ventoux (covering a quarter of the area) and the Coteaux-de-Pierrevert (covering half of it). Although the Côtes-du-Lubéron appellation spreads across more than 15,000 acres (6,000 hectares), the area of vineyards in production covers 9,847 acres (3,987 hectares) along the Lubéron chain. The appellation is contiguous with the Côtes-du-Ventoux, which is why numerous growers and cooperatives make wines for both appellations.

As for the types of wine made, 60 percent are reds, 20 percent whites, and 20 percent rosés. In the Lubéron, the red wines have a lot of character, being both sensuous and robust, smooth yet heady, with aromas of dark berries, pepper, truffles, leather, and undergrowth. These are wines for the fall and winter, marrying well with highly flavored foods such as beef stew and game. The whites are fresh, crisp, aromatic, and elegant, with dominant notes of peach, apricot, linden blossom, and honeysuckle. They are the ideal accompaniment to broiled or grilled fish and goat cheese. Strong, expressive, and generous, the rosés are surprisingly fresh with a red-berry nose. Their structure allows them to be drunk as aperitifs or with a meal, especially with white meat, saddle of lamb, baby stuffed

vegetables, and slightly spicy dishes. In the case of the best wines, the whites and rosés should be kept for three to five years, five to ten years for the reds. The latter should ideally be served at 52°F (14°C), the whites at 44°F to 50°F (8°C to 10°C), and the rosés at 50°F to 53°F (10°C to 12°C).

For the reds and rosés, the permitted grape varieties are Syrah, Grenache, Mourvèdre, Carignan, and Cinsault, as well as a few secondary varieties such as Picpoul Noir, Counoise Noire, Gamay Noir, and Pinot Noir. Syrah, with its ruby color and wild fragrances, contributes to the roundness and finesse of the red wines. Grenache supplies high alcoholic content, as well as fruit aromas, and Cinsault tempers the strength of Grenache by adding finesse. As for the whites, Grenache Blanc, recognizable from its pale greenish-yellow color and powerful, floral nose, contributes roundness, alcoholic strength, and delicate fragrances. Ugni Blanc, pale lemon in color, brings acidity and backbone. Vigorous, tasty Vermentino only became a permitted variety in the appellation in 1990. Blended with Grenache Blanc, it contributes fullness and a syrupy, ripe-fruit flavor. Clairette Blanc, which grows well in poor, dry soils, is one of the oldest varieties recorded in Provence. It produces wines that are high in alcohol with a fruity aroma. Bourboulenc is not widely used, but it produces fresh, aromatic wines of a floral character. Roussanne and Marsanne are used as secondary varieties.

A LITTLE HISTORY

The Romans came to this fortunate region in 124 B.C., almost exactly a year after they had settled in Marseille. The Rhône valley between Montélimar and Arles was shaped by the Roman field sys-

CHÂTEAU DE MILLE, THE SUMMER RESIDENCE OF POPE CLEMENT V, IS BELIEVED TO BE ONE OF THE OLDEST WINE ESTATES IN THE LUBÉRON. THE RED WINE PRODUCED HERE HAS A DEEP CRIMSON COLOR AND A NOSE OF RED CURRANT, EUCALYPTUS, AND BAY LEAF. ITS STRONG CHARACTER MIRRORS THAT OF ITS ILLUSTRIOUS FORMER OWNER.

tem known as "centuriation," in which the land was divided up into squares measuring around 2,330 feet (710 meters) on each side. These blocks of land were allocated to the bravest legionaries for their retirement. If you climb to the hilltop village of Bonnieux, the checkerboard effect of centuriation can be clearly seen in the geometric regularity of the vineyards. There are a number of other vestiges of Roman occupation, as can be seen at places like Château Val Joanis, built on the foundations of a Roman villa, the fountain and cascades of Château La Canorgue, and the pottery kiln at Château Grand Callamand. In 906, the bishop of Apt donated vines to Bonnieux and in 1428, the consuls of the village La Bastide des Jourdans prohibited the sale of wine that had been mixed with water. In the eighteenth century, vines covered 18 percent of the land around the village of Lourmarin and 30 percent of the land around La Tour d'Aigues. The vineyard flourished from the late nineteenth century until the interwar period, thanks to the creation of the first cooperatives. In 1951, the Côtes-du-Lubéron were granted Vin Délimité de Qualité Supérieure status. It was not until the 1970s, however, that the winemakers, conscious of the need to modernize, began making substantial investments. Their efforts were crowned with success in 1988 when the Côtes-du-Lubéron became an Appellation d'Origine Contrôlée for white, red, and rosé wines.

ITINERARY

Ménerbes, which sits on its clifftop overlooking the vineyards like the prow of a ship, can claim to be one of the most beautiful villages in France. In 1992, Yves Rousset-Rouard, a successful film producer, decided to turn his hand to winemaking, building a cellar at the foot of the village where he already owned a vacation home.

He attended a sale of corkscrews at the Hôtel Drouot, the famous Paris auction house, without knowing anything about them and became caught up in the bidding, buying 80 percent of the collection, around a hundred items. They range from old designs dating back as far as the eighteenth century to veritable works of art made from ivory and silver, as well as humorous pieces. This budding collector subsequently decided to open a corkscrew museum on the site of his vineyard at Domaine de la Citadelle as a homage to the humble yet little-known implement. His vines cover an area of 109 acres (44 hectares), of which eighty-one acres (thirty-three hectares) are in the appellation and twenty-seven acres (eleven hectares) are used for making Vin de Pays de Vaucluse. All are planted on a north-facing slope, making it possible to create wines of great complexity and finesse, such as the Cuvée Noé in honor of the owner's grandson or the Cuvée du Gouverneur, a wine that will continue improving in the bottle for ten years. Both wines are made from old vines of Syrah and, in smaller quantities, Grenache.

About a mile from the village on the road to Bonnieux stands the Bastide de Marie, an eighteenth-century fortified farmhouse surrounded by vines. It once belonged to the female owner of a Paris fashion house, but was converted into a guesthouse by Jocelyne and Jean-Louis Sibuet who are well known in Parisian interior design circles. They had barely moved in when Jean-Louis succumbed to the temptation of making his own wine. His rosé is a great success. For his wine called Le, he selects the finest grapes, using 90 percent Grenache and 10 percent Syrah from vines whose average age is thirty-five years. Only 3,500 bottles of this dense, aromatic wine are made each year. The vineyard occupies three different *terroirs*, covering about fifty acres (twenty hectares). This diversity makes it possible to juggle the subtle differences in the aromas of grapes from each

THE SIBUET FAMILY, FAMOUS HOTELIERS FROM THE SKI RESORT OF MÉGÈVE, HAVE FALLEN IN LOVE WITH THE VILLAGE OF MÉNERBES, WHERE THEY HAVE RESTORED A FARMHOUSE KNOWN AS THE BASTIDE DE MARIE (FACING PAGE).
IT IS EXQUISITELY DECORATED IN THE PROVENÇAL STYLE AND PRODUCES A ROSÉ, A WHITE, AND TWO RED WINES OF IMPECCABLE QUALITY (LEFT).
VAL JOANIS IS AN ESTATE THAT IS AS FAMOUS FOR ITS WINES AS FOR ITS MAGNIFICENT SIXTEENTH-CENTURY MANSION, RESTORED IN THE NINETEENTH CENTURY, AND BEAUTIFUL GARDENS. THE RED KNOWN AS LES GRIOTTES, WITH ITS NOSE OF LICORICE, PEPPER, AND BERRIES, IS THE JEWEL IN THE CROWN OF THE APPELLATION (FOLLOWING DOUBLE PAGE).

plot. The wines are aged in a wonderful *chai*, which can be viewed through a window from what is the most decorative and original tasting room in the whole of the Lubéron.

Château La Canorgue is in nearby Bonnieux and offers spectacular views over the plain of Cavalon and Mont Ventoux. La Canorgue is built on the foundations of an ancient Roman villa and gets its name from the numerous underground channels, often cut into the rock, that the Romans built for carrying water. These excavations are still in use and are one of the estate's proudest features. With its seventeenth-century façade, this is the most elegant château in the Lubéron. Designed as a summer residence, it has a huge terrace shaded with plane trees overlooking the vines and a fountain that is often used in summer for cooling wine bottles. The house has a typically Provençal air of easy living about it. The owner, Jean-Pierre Margan, is an inveterate traveler and if he is not busy driving across a desert in a 4X4, he might, if you are lucky, receive you in the huge tasting cellar, where he is likely to be accompanied by his dog Merlot

or his intrepid daughter, Nathalie. The wine made here are so good and so well known that it is not unusual to meet a French movie star, politician, or media personality who has dropped by to purchase a case or two. Jean-Pierre Margan converted the vineyard to organic production in 1980, although he does not use this as a selling point. His main aim is to produce wines that are as natural as possible, using organic and biodynamic methods. The vineyards are cared for with natural products and according to the astral cycles. Jean-Pierre Margan embarked on his winemaking enterprise in 1976, when he planted the major varieties of the appellation, and his relentless labor was rewarded in 1979 when he won a medal for his first wine. The vines cover about ninety-eight acres (forty hectares) of land sur rounding the property. The rather poor soil is a mixture of clay and limestone strewn with pebbles, and the yields are low, at about 320 gallons an acre (thirty hectoliters a hectare). The red, white, and rosé Vendanges de Nathalie, made by the owner's daughter, are all excellent.

After Bonnieux, the vines give way to the *garrigue* and evergreen oaks. From here, the visitor can either go south in the direction of Lourmarin, or north toward Apt, capital of the Lubéron. This second route takes you to the Château de Mille. When the D3, which links Bonnieux and Apt, begins to zigzag through forest, then you are almost there. Make a left along a potholed road and you will find yourself in front of the large twelfth-century feudal residence. In this delightful oasis of nature covering 370 acres (150 hectares) lies one of the oldest and most unusual vineyards in the region, with an area of 125 acres (50 hectares). With its machicolations and loophole windows for shooting arrows, this fairytale castle looks like a child's cardboard cutout. It osriginally served as the summer residence of Pope Clement V, and was owned by the bishops of Apt. It was built on a stone plinth cut out of the rock, as can be seen in the uneven inner courtyard. The medieval vats and a wine press are also carved out of the rock, evidence that the Château de Mille has made wine throughout its existence. Such an unusual setting requires an unusual owner. Conrad Pinatel, the current proprietor of the estate, which has belonged to the same family since 1780, is a colorful and talkative character and is particularly entertaining when recounting the estate's recent history. It was part of the Côtes-du-Rhône appellation from 1916 to 1939, before being transferred to the Côtes-de-Provence and then the Côtes-du-Ventoux appellations, and finally that of the Côtes-du-Luberon. That is why he once wrote on a wine label, "Regimes pass, appellations change, quality remains!" This larger-than-life mustachioed ambassador for the wines of Lubéron inspects his vines on horseback, collects tasting cups, and produces wines very much in his own image. They are typical of their appellation, possessing body, strength, and nobility, with a touch of wildness. The red wine is vinified in the traditional manner, being aged for a long time in a huge oak vat holding 3,900 gallons (150 hectoliters) to prevent oxidation. This dark red has won numerous medals and the owner recommends serving it in the same way as a great Burgundy.

Château Val Joanis is located between Pertuis and Villelaure on the D973. It is as famous for its formal garden, with its terraces, kitchen garden, flower beds, bowers, and pergolas, as it is for its wine. It also has a great farm store that sells all kinds of delightful Provençal goods. Jean-Louis Chancel came across the estate in 1977. It lies on the site of a Roman villa and has managed to survive various upheavals without losing any of its land, remaining exactly the same size as it was when Cassini surveyed it in 1575. However, in the nineteenth century it fell into disrepair and lost some of its luster. A massive restoration campaign was launched in 1979. Ditches were dug to drain away the water, and the slopes were restored to revive the soil that is strewn with round pebbles. Architect Jean-Jacques Pichoux designed buildings covered in old tiles to contain cellars full of barrels and air-conditioned storage areas. At the same time, Cécile Chancel, with the help of landscape gardener Tobbie Loup de Viane, created three terraces of gardens around the château to curb the ocean of vines that cover 1,000 acres (400 hectares) of the estate, although less than 150 acres (60 hectares) are devoted to the production of appellation wines. The Chancel family's philosophy is to protect the environment so as to leave future generations more than it has received—hence their policy of low yields and sensible cultivation. Their flagship wine is the Les Griottes red made from Grenache and Syrah. This rich, well-rounded wine, with its ripe berry and plum flavors with a hint of pepper, bears the name of the plot of land at the highest point of the property, nearly 1,640 feet (500 meters) above sea level.

DOMAINE DE LA CITADELLE
2003
EN BOUTEILLE AU DOMAINE
PROPRIÉTAIRES RÉCOLTANTS A 84560 MÉNERBES-FRANCE

VIOGNIER
VIN DE PAYS DE VAUCLUSE

PRODUCE OF FRANCE

DOMAINE DE LA CITADELLE

CÔTES DU LUBERON
APPELLATION CÔTES DU LUBERON CONTRÔLÉE

2003
MIS EN BOUTEILLE AU DOMAINE
Y. ROUSSET-ROUARD & FILS
PROPRIÉTAIRES RÉCOLTANTS A 84560 MÉNERBES-FRANCE

Cuvée du Gou
DOMAINE DE LA CI

CÔTES DU LUBERON
APPELLATION CÔTES DU LUBERON CONTRÔLÉE

2000
MIS EN BOUTEILLE AU DOMAINE
Y. ROUSSET-ROUARD & FILS
PROPRIÉTAIRES RÉCOLTANTS A 84560 MÉNERBES-FRANCE

PRODUCT OF FRANCE

PROVENCE AND CORSICA

The vines of Domaine Richeaume cover the lower slopes
of Mont Sainte-Victoire, the famous landmark much painted
by Cézanne. The vines are cultivated organically and the
wines, aged in new oak, are full-bodied and vigorous.

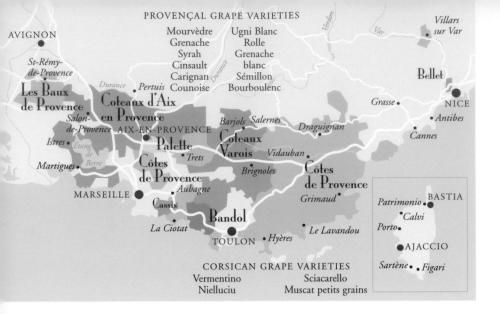

PROVENÇAL GRAPE VARIETIES
Mourvèdre   Ugni Blanc
Grenache   Rolle
Syrah   Grenache
Cinsault   blanc
Carignan   Sémillon
Counoise   Bourboulenc

CORSICAN GRAPE VARIETIES
Vermentino   Sciacarello
Nielluciu   Muscat petits grains

PROVENCE AND CORSICA: WINES WHOSE TEMPERAMENT MATCHES THAT OF THE WINEMAKERS

Provence is a multifaceted region, a compendium of contradictory clichés. Inland, in the *arrière-pays*, life is slow, rural, and peaceful, rooted in tradition; on the coast it is fast, cosmopolitan, and superficial. The region's idiosyncrasies are sometimes endearing, but frequently irritating. Picturesque Provençal villages have traveled the world on postcards, but this is also the land of inflated prices, Hollywood-style swimming pools, palm trees, honey-colored skies, and gentle hills crowned by twisted cypress limbs reaching for the sky just as van Gogh painted them. Long lines of grape vines clad the slopes, the flourishing emblem of a countryside in which architecture and landscape merge seamlessly. In spite of everything, Provence, land of fruits and sunshine, remains a magical place—magnetic, rich, and enchanting. It will always have a romanticism capable of melting the hardest of hearts.

The largest appellation in the region—indeed in France—is Côtes-de-Provence, which covers 36,500 acres (14,700 hectares). It extends from the outskirts of Marseille to the southern flanks of the Mont Sainte-Victoire, taking in the islands of Hyères, the Massif des Maures with its prestigious vacation resorts, the lands north of Draguignan, and the little enclave around Villars, north of Nice. In addition, there are the Coteaux d'Aix-en-Provence, 9,500 acres (3,800 hectares), planted along the banks of the Durance, at the foot of the Alpilles, and south toward the sea.

The tiny appellation of Les Baux-de-Provence, wedged between the Coteaux d'Aix and the Rhône appellations, is named after the village of the same name, which remains as picturesque as ever despite the legions of backpackers and holidaymakers who now throng the streets. It is buffeted by the merciless mistral wind from the north, but caressed by mild sea breezes. Les Baux opted very early for quality and has been almost completely converted to organic cultivation. Provence also boasts the newly formed enclave of Coteaux du Varois, further to the north, an appellation covering 3,890 acres (1,575 hectares) where winemakers use grape varieties that are unknown elsewhere, such as Tibouren and Calitor.

The distinguished vineyards of Bandol extend over 3,000 acres (1,200 hectares) between luxury resorts and picture postcard villages with brightly painted façades. Cassis, the small, old port to the east of Marseille, has its own 400-acre (160-hectare) appellation and could teach many other white wine producers a thing or two. As for the Bellet appellation, its ninety-four acres (thirty-eight hectares) continue to battle bravely against the encroaching property developers. Cooled by winds from the sea and the mountains, its producers prefer Italian grape varieties such as Braquet (Brachetto) and Folle Noire. Finally, to the east of Aix-en-Provence, there is the smallest (fifty acres [twenty hectares]) yet most prestigious appellation in the region: Palette. Here Château Simone, despite northern exposure, has been producing remarkable wines for two hundred years.

THE ATTRACTIVE WHITE WINES IN CHÂTEAU REVELETTE'S CHÂTEAU LINE SHOULD BE DRUNK WHEN THEY ARE YOUNG AND AT THEIR MOST FRUITY.
THEY ARE AMONG THE MOST RELIABLE WINES OF THE COTEAUX D'AIX-EN-PROVENCE APPELLATION.

Each of these appellations produces delightful reds, rosés, and whites that can offer extraordinary variations in character. There are strong, fruity, luscious reds (Côtes-de-Provence, Coteaux d'Aix-en-Provence, Coteaux du Varois, and Coteaux de Pierrevert); reds that are aged in barrels and intended for laying down (Bandol, Baux-de-Provence, Côtes-de-Provence, and Coteaux d'Aix-en-Provence); dry, lively, aromatic rosés with floral bouquets and notes of thyme, juniper, and resin (Côtes-de-Provence, Coteaux de Varois, Coteaux-d'Aix, and Bandol), or even of heather (Massif des Maures); and whites that have been aged in barrels so they are deep, rounded, supple, and fruity (Palette, Cassis, Bandol, Côtes-de-Provence, and Bellet).

As for Corsica, it offers rare wines made from grape varieties that are to be found nowhere else. Home to as many as nine Appellations d'Origine Contrôlée, it is a place of extraordinary diversity. In this land of *dolce vita*, where in August and September it rains six times less than in the Bordeaux region and the sun shines six hundred hours more, the wines deserve to be savored sip by sip rather than guzzled. Although still little known, Corsican wines have improved down the years and are no longer rustic concoctions suitable only for summer drinking. The reds tend to be full-bodied, tannic, and high in alcohol, with aromas that conjure up the *maquis*, spices, and red berries. In short, these are wines for people who enjoy pleasant surprises.

In this region tailor-made for lazing, vacationing, and sharing a leisurely meal with friends, the Provençal rosé has long been the adult version of pink lemonade. Yet even though more than 70 percent of rosés remain mere thirst-quenchers, an increasing number of winemakers have learned how to create more sophisticated blends in which Cinsault is the predominant variety. Easy to make and drink but hard to get exactly right, these delicate wines account for 80 percent of total production in both good years and bad. Unfairly disparaged because little known, this wine embodies all the seductive hedonism of Provence, containing a symphony of colors ranging from rose petal to fuchsia through shot silk.

Wines in regions highly popular with tourists are rarely inexpensive, and this is certainly true of Provence, where good value for money is hard to come by. But visitors are entitled to give themselves a treat from time to time without paying too much attention to labels. At such times, the sumptuous reds and wonderfully fresh whites of the Côtes-du-Lubéron at the northern edge of Provence fit the bill perfectly. Besides, as the French say, when you are in love, you don't count the cost.

AT CASSIS, THE VINES SEEM TO BE IMPREGNATED WITH
THE AROMAS OF THE GARRIGUE AND THE SEA BREEZES
THAT BLOW IN FROM THE NEARBY MEDITERRANEAN.

BANDOL:
THE SPIRIT OF MOURVÈDRE

Provence has a wild, rugged beauty. Dreamlike villages dot the fluid, rolling landscape across which the vines clear a path, elbowing their way through the thick *garrigue*. The grapes here seem to be impregnated with the fragrance and tranquility of the surrounding biotope. The Bandol vineyards face full south toward the Mediterranean, infected by the same relaxed, leisurely mood that pervades the rest of the region. Dotted with olive and almond trees, the land is shaped into a natural amphitheater here, creating a microclimate and sheltering the vines from sudden changes in weather. A subtle balance of breezes from seaward and landward operates: the mistral, the keen north wind, has a cooling effect, while the breezes that blow from the east and southeast bring refreshing rains that leapfrog from the mountains to the sea. In short, the vine has found a location of great rarity here. In order to grow vines on the steep slopes, the growers have had to carve terraces out of the mountainside, shoring them up with drystone walls known as *restanques*. For several generations, the local farmers have labored to remove the stones from the land by hand to create these long drystone terraces, which follow the curve of the mountains and require constant maintenance in order to protect them from erosion.

This tiny appellation lies in very arid territory, occupying an area of 3,420 acres (1,384 hectares) divided between eight *communes* in the cantons of Ollioules and Beausset, northwest of Toulon. Created in 1941, the appellation is one of the oldest in France. Production is limited by decree to forty hectoliters per hectare (427 gallons per acre), but the producers—fifty independents and five cooperatives—restrict themselves to considerably less for reasons of quality, and the yield generally does not exceed thirty-five hectoliters per hectare (374 gallons per acre).

In this most unusual *place*, the most successful blends are achieved using Mourvèdre. It is a vine whose grapes are difficult to mature; they ripen late and the yield is low. In Bandol it has been received as a godsend, but other appellations have been put off by the ripening difficulties. Mourvèdre, Grenache, Cinsault, and, as secondary varieties, Syrah and Carignan are all used to enrich the palette of reds and rosés. In the case of Bandol reds, the winemaker's patience is richly rewarded. Oak-aged for eighteen months, these are serious wines intended for laying down, becoming drinkable only after five or six years. The color of dark pomegranate, they are rich, elegant, and well rounded, bursting with flavors of Morello cherry, mulberry, black currant, and raspberry. The rosés, which are best drunk young, are pleasant wines that combine charm, freshness, and depth. Supple, fruity, and very dry, they are the result of direct pressings. The whites, of which few are produced, are made from Clairette, Ugni Blanc, and Bourboulenc, together with a small amount of Sauvignon Blanc. They develop aromas of hazelnut, almond, hawthorn, and citrus. In the mouth they are fresh and lively, with a delicate palette of flavors.

ITINERARY

The Domaine de Frégate covers the *communes* of Saint-Cyr-sur-Mer and Bandol, its vines growing around the rocky creek known as the Calanque de Port-d'Alon. The view is so spectacular that a four-star hotel and a twenty-seven-hole golf course have opted to share it. Its location, on a promontory open to the south and west, provides the seventy-nine acres (thirty-two hectares) of vines with exceptional exposure to the sun, enabling the grapes to ripen uniformly. The estate has been owned by the same family for three generations and makes mainly reds and rosés, together with a small amount of white. It is possible to sample its pleasant, fruity wines in the attractive tasting cellar, but a better option is to have a meal on the terrace of the restaurant, savoring a bottle or two of the estate's wines while enjoying the panoramic view.

FOR THREE GENERATIONS, THE OTT FAMILY HAS BEEN MAKING SUCCESSFUL WINES IN THREE APPELLATIONS. THE COEUR DE GRAIN IS THE ROSÉ OF STARS AND A STAR AMONG ROSÉS. ITS ROUNDNESS AND SUPPLENESS MAKE IT THE IDEAL COMPANION TO EXOTIC DISHES AND PROVENÇAL COOKING, AND IT FEATURES ON THE WINE LISTS OF THE MOST PRESTIGIOUS RESTAURANTS.

To reach Château Pibarnon you follow a long, winding road offering elegant glimpses of the Bec de l'Aigle ("Eagle's Beak") outcrop and the Embiez mountains. The château stands on the Colline du Télégraphe ("Telegraph Hill"), where the old telegraph relay station that linked Toulon with Paris once stood, overlooking the highest vineyards in Bandol. The handsome property, with its green shutters and wrought-iron balconies, has views over the whole vineyard and takes in the picturesque villages of La Cadière and Le Castellet. Henri and Catherine de Saint-Victor discovered the 1975 Château Pibarnon red during a lunch one day and it was love at first sip. They became so enthusiastic about the wine that they decided to visit the property, which lies one thousand feet above sea level and has breathtaking views of the hills and the Mediterranean. In the foreground, the landscape is dotted with cypresses and shrubs, and in the distance the vines are planted on terraces around a natural depression, forming a sort of hanging garden. The Saint-Victors bought a parcel of forty acres (sixteen hectares), of which less than a quarter is planted with vines. No cellarmaster? No matter, Henri would take charge of the winemaking. No vineyard manager? The intrepid count would drive the tractor himself. No customers for the wine? The couple toured the local restaurants and wine merchants themselves to present their wines. The vineyard was too small? This former CEO of a patenting and licensing company rolled up his sleeves and cleared the land, terracing and planting another fifteen acres (six hectares). After this Herculean effort, the first wines, made in 1978, were a triumph. The red and the rosé both won gold medals, while the white won a silver medal. Without realizing it, Henri and Catherine de Saint-Victor had acquired an exceptional vineyard, for the soil here is quite different from that of the rest of the appellation. Fortune smiled on the couple again when they were given the opportunity to purchase the cirque opposite the cellar. After months of bulldozing, they discovered a layer of blue soil that turned out to be Santonian marl, the same subsoil that is found in the vineyards of such classic wines as Pétrus, Yquem, and Château Chalon. The Pibarnon reds consist of 90 to 95 percent Mourvèdre, the variety that is the mainstay of Bandol wines. When young, they are very aromatic, with a bouquet of hawthorn, mulberry, and violet, supplemented later by notes of licorice and pepper. However, it takes five years of cellaring before these full-bodied, rich, elegant wines are really drinkable. And after ten years of lying forgotten in the dust, they taste of berries, with floral fragrances reminiscent of peonies or heliotropes and hints of undergrowth, truffles, spices, cinnamon, or musk. They are perfect accompaniments to the seasonal foods of autumn and the gourmet delights of Christmas. The house rosé, which has a lovely coral color, is also delicious. Made from Mourvèdre and Cinsault, it has power and refinement, finesse and exuberance, with a velvety, silky texture. It is the perfect accompaniment to local dishes and also makes a great aperitif.

The star of the rosés is also the rosé of the stars. The rosé made by the Château de Romassan, one of the prestigious Domaines d'Ott, has made regular appearances in the pages of celebrity gossip magazines down the years. From Jean Cocteau to James Bond, to say nothing of the starlets promenading the Croisette in Cannes and the models in Saint-Tropez, this rosé is the favorite tipple. There's not a fashionable establishment or Michelin-starred restaurant on the Côte d'Azur that does not include it in the wine list. Its sucess is merited. This illustrious rosé is made at the foot of the village of Le Castellet. In 1956, the vineyard was bought by Marcel Ott, who came from Alsace and already owned Château de Selle and Clos Mireille in the Côtes-de-Provence. With its saffron walls and olive-green shutters, the handsome, eighteenth-century château confers grandeur on the surrounding countryside. After tasting the wines, it is well worth visiting the beautiful vaulted wine cellars. This 148-acre (60 hectare) property has been entirely replanted during the last thirty years.

And adding to the charm of the location is a delightful little dry stone chapel in the midst of the vines. The wine is the result of the combination of an exceptional location and unusual working methods. The vines are trained on trellises, a rarity in this region, and the grapes are harvested by hand and carefully sorted, with fermentation taking place in temperature-controlled vats. The result is a rosé with an inimitably spicy flavor. The prestigious Cuvée Marcel Ott is aged in oak barrels for eight to ten months, producing a full rosé with a fruity note of peach. This is a rosé that can be aged in your own wine cellar and drunk several years later. It goes particularly well with foie gras or the finest cured meats. As for the Cœur de Grain rosé, which is full and round, fruity and sensual, it is quite simply incomparable.

Château Vannières lies between the villages of La Cadière-d'Azur and Saint-Cyr-sur-Mer, and is protected from the north wind by the Sainte-Baume mountains. In 1957, the grandfather of the present owner acquired the estate as a gift for his daughter. Today, Eric Boisseaux has taken over running of the property from his mother.

With its brick and stone façades, the château resembles a castle in Flanders, but with a Genoese touch in the form of the square tower with flat roof. The total area of the land is 116 acres (47 hectares), eighty-two acres (thirty-three hectares) of which are planted with the traditional varieties of the Bandol and Côtes-de-Provence appellations. The average age of the vines is thirty-five years. Although traditional cultivation techniques are used, the reds are matured in oak casks and the rosés and whites in stainless steel vats. The marl and limestone soil gives the wines balance and elegance, with a powerful bouquet and refined tannins. Château Vannières maintains a respect for traditional winemaking practice, while making use of modern techniques. The estate sells two wines dating from as long ago as 1979, as well as Vins de Pays du Mont-Caume. The Vannières red, with its delicious fragrances of black currant and blueberries and background notes of pepper and spices, goes well with garlic-flavored roast lamb or duck with olives. This is one of the subtlest reds of an appellation that—whatever the winemakers of Bordeaux may say—can be reminiscent of a fine claret from Pauillac.

BAUX DE PROVENCE:
SIGNATURE ORGANIC WINES

The name Baux de Provence conjures up pristine natural beauty, bucolic pleasure, idyllic vacations, hazy sunlight, and the fragrance of the *garrigue* wafting on the breeze. This wine-growing area lies to the northwest of Aix-en-Provence, on the northern and southern slopes of the Alpilles, a range of diminutive mountains thirty kilometers long running east to west. There are only fourteen vineyards in this pocket-size appellation, which was only created in 1995. The estates nestle discreetly among the hills, at the end of long dirt paths, and the visitor is usually guaranteed a pleasant experience in the form of an enthusiastic winemaker, a glass of wine, a moment of conviviality—in short, life at its simplest.

Wedged between two olive groves, the vineyards cover an area of 993 acres (402 hectares) that includes eight villages on the northern and southern slopes of the Alpilles: Fontvieille, Les Baux, Le Paradou, Maussane, Mouriès, Eygalières, Saint-Rémy-de-Provence, and Saint-Étienne-du-Grès. The plateau of Les Baux towers over the stony Crau plain like the prow of a ship, offering views of Vaccarès and the sea. The vineyards are sheltered by pine forests and bluish boulders, and the wines are the product of an approach that combines tradition and science, with low yields, an extended growing season, and in some cases organic or biodynamic methods. As a result, the wines have found favor with connoisseurs and previously little-known estates have been linked with the heavily starred masters of French cuisine. The Vins des Baux appellation only covers red and rosé wines, the white wines coming within the Coteaux d'Aix appellation. The Institut National des Appellations d'Origine (INAO) is considering plans to recognize a future appellation called Vins des Baux en Blanc. With this in mind, winemakers have suggested introducing the Marsanne and Roussane varieties.

An unparalleled 85 percent of the vines in the Baux de Provence appellation are grown organically, which explains why the yields are so low, at only thirty-two hectoliters per hectare (342 gallons per acre). This choice illustrates the philosophy of the local winemakers, who like to take their time in making their wines. Indeed, the average amount of time they allow for the reds to mature has been increasing every year since the appellation was created. The picturesque vineyard consists of 71 percent red grape varieties, 21.5 percent rosé, and 7.5 percent white. Grenache, Syrah, and Mourvèdre represent at least 60 percent of the vine stocks, while Cinsault, Counoise, Carignan, and Cabernet Sauvignon are used as secondary varieties. The wines are hearty, robust, and tannic. When young, aromas of rosemary and tobacco dominate, developing into dark berry or animal notes of amber and game. The reds have always needed to age for around a year, but since the creation of the appellation, this period could profitably be extended to around eighteen months. The rosés consist of a minimum of 60 percent Grenache and Syrah, used in combination with the secondary varieties of Mourvèdre, Carignan, and Counoise. These solid but rustic rosés are fruity and floral, with burnt understones.

ITINERARY

The winemakers of the Vallée des Baux also cultivate olive trees. At the Château d'Estoublon the olive and the grape share the limelight. This handsome eighteenth-century property, which stands guard at the entrance to the village of Fontvieille, on the southern slopes of the Alpilles, has 500 acres (200 hectares) of land, 118 acres (48 hectares) of them planted with olive trees and forty-two acres (seventeen hectares) with vines. Both vineyards and olive groves have appellation classification. The history of the château is inseparable from that of the Vallée des Baux, of which it is one of the most

THE CELLAR AT CHÂTEAU ROMANIN HAS BEEN CARVED OUT OF THE ROCK AND LOOKS LIKE
A SHRINE TO BACCHUS, THE GOD OF WINE. THE PUREST CONCENTRATES OF THE TERROIR ARE
VINIFIED HERE, THE YARDSTICK AGAINST WHICH OTHER WINES OF THE APPELLATION ARE MEASURED.

impressive sights. In January 1999, Estoublon was purchased by the Schneider family, who then spent three years refurbishing the estate. Everything, from cellar to reception room, received a makeover, and two charming stores were added selling local produce and decorative items. Valérie, the charming owner with a passion for interior design, has made every effort to create an atmosphere that combines two influences: that of her homeland, Switzerland, and that of Provence, her adoptive region. The vineyards are overseen by Rémy Reboul, the son-in-law of the house, who has been helped by Éloi Dürrbach, the generous owner of the Domaine de Trévallon. For five years, these two men worked hard together on the land, restructuring the soil, replacing old varieties with new ones, introducing organic methods, and building a new wine cellar. The energy expended was as great as the amount of money spent. The replanting of red varieties conformed to the requirements of the appellation, but in the white grape areas Rémy and Éloi decided to plant Marsanne and Roussane, two varieties that are not recognized by the Coteaux d'Aix appellation. The result is a wine that has remarkable finesse and freshness. If you do not have time to climb up to the Cité des Baux to enjoy the panoramic view of the valley, you can always admire the rocky landscape from the

Mas Sainte-Berthe. The view of the château from there is stunning. One thing is for sure, it is impossible to pass by the property without noticing it, since its vines cover the land on either side of the road than leads down to Saint-Rémy and Maussane.

Art lovers who are also wine lovers should not miss the Mas de la Dame, which was painted by Vincent van Gogh. The Mas de la Dame, located at the foot of the Baux de Provence outcrop, on the southern slope of the Alpilles, has one of the best views of the Alpilles and Les Baux. The property was purchased in the 1930s by the grandfather of the two current owners and was the first commercial vineyard and olive grove in the district. The land covers a continuous area of 750 acres (300 hectares), of which 142 acres (57 hectares) are planted with vines and sixty-seven acres (twenty-seven hectares) with olive trees. The farmhouse was painted by van Gogh in 1889 during his stay in Saint-Rémy-de-Provence, but unfortunately the canvas, entitled *A Farmhouse on the Road to Saint-Rémy*, was stolen from its American owner in the 1960s and has never been recovered. All the south-facing plots of land have a dry, wind-blown climate with plenty of sunshine that concentrates the juice in the grapes. Anne Poniatowski and Caroline Missoffe wanted

to breathe new life into their wines and called in the enologist Jean-Luc Colombo, whose reputation extends way beyond his native village of Cornas. Experiments were conducted to gain a better understanding of the vineyards, certain plots were selected, the yields were reduced, and manual harvesting was adopted. This policy resulted in such exceptional *cuvées* as Le Coin Caché, La Stèle, and Le Vallon des Amants.

The next stop is Domaine Hauvette. Take the road to Saint-Rémy-de-Provence, and then the Voie Aurélia (the old Roman road), which branches off after the Fondation Prassinos. It is advisable to go slowly here, as the road is dangerously narrow and your attention is likely be distracted by the magnificent scenery. After the right-hand fork leading to La Galine, you will reach the Domaine Hauvette, where on no account should you drop in unannounced. Dominique Hauvette, one of the three women winemakers of the appellation, does everything entirely alone, from tending the vines to cellaring. After your visit, go back along the road you came on and take a right along the Voie Aurélia. Follow the cart track that starts right in front of the aerodrome runway, and which leads to the Château Romanin, it's all well signposted. For those who enjoy walking, this section makes a

wonderful hike. You have the feeling you are walking to the end of the world. Even if it seems like a long way, resist the temptation to turn back, because it will be a good few miles before you reach the door of the cellar, where you will be received by the chef and owner of the Oustau-de-Baumanières restaurant. Each year a special wine is made at Château Romanin using the estate's best grapes. Called Le Coeur de Château Romanin, this range of high-quality wines is only made in small quantities. In 1998, for example, there were only nine hundred bottles of Primus, while in 2001 only eight thousand bottles of Quartus were produced. The château also makes a delicious, lively red known as La Chapelle de Romanin.

When you leave this magical place you will have to retrace your steps until you reach the crossroads, then take the dirt road to the Domaine des Terres Blanches. If you prefer walking on level ground this is the time to get a little fresh air. A pretty little path runs

THE BAUX DE PROVENCE APPELLATION IS NAMED
AFTER THE FORTRESS BUILT ON A ROCKY SPUR
IN THE HEART OF THE ALPILLES. THE VINES CLING
TO THIS PLATEAU 816 FEET (245 METERS) ABOVE SEA LEVEL.

THE WINES OF DOMAINE DE TRÉVALLON (BELOW) ARE
ONLY CLASSIFIED AS VINS DE PAYS DES BOUCHES DU RHÔNE
BECAUSE THE BLENDS DO NOT CONFORM TO APPELLATION
SPECIFICATIONS, BUT THEY ARE AVIDLY SOUGHT BY
COLLECTORS THROUGHOUT THE WORLD.
MAS DE LA DAME (FACING PAGE) IS MUCH OLDER. ONE OF
THE REGION'S MORE TRADITIONAL AND EXTENSIVE WINE
ESTATES, IT WAS IMMORTALIZED BY VAN GOGH IN A PAINTING.
ITS REDS, SUCH AS LE COIN CACHÉ, ARE POWERFUL
WINES WITH DELIGHTFUL AROMAS OF UNDERGROWTH.

through a grove of pine trees for nearly one and a quarter miles. Behind the pines lies one of the best-preserved vineyards in the Alpilles. It is also a good lesson in grape varieties, because each plot is labeled with a wooden marker indicating the variety planted.

The story of the Domaine des Terres Blanches began in 1968 when Noël Michelin decided to restore the 150 acres (60 hectares) of land he had just bought on a north-facing slope of the Alpilles. A true visionary, he invested in organic farming, elected to conserve a large part of the native scrubland, the *garrigue*, where live oaks, almond trees, and olive trees contributed to the very specific ecology surrounding the one hundred acres (forty hectares) of vines, protecting them from the violence of the mistral from the north. At Terres Blanches, polyculture is an important feature of land management. Unless there is a drought, the grass grows symbiotically with the vines. The presence of this wild vegetation makes it possible to maintain the necessary harmony and cohabitation between fauna and flora. Insects and spiders are treated as friends rather than foe here: "Some of them indeed feed at the expense of the vines, but others feed at the expense of the former, the rest just sit back and keep score," comments Guillaume Rerolle, the late Noël Michelin's son-in-law. The soil is fed with a simple homemade vegetable compost and if the vine needs protecting from fungal parasites such as mildew, the owner uses natural pest controls such as Bordeaux mixture (copper sulfate), sulfur, seaweed, plant extracts—and the mistral. The rosé, one of the best of the appellation, is delightful. It is made from 40 percent Grenache, 30 percent Mourvèdre, and 30 percent Counoise. With its pink color, enhanced with purple reflections, its delightful nose developing into fragrances of citrus, red currant, and white-fleshed fruits, it has wonderful balance and a lively, fruity flavor. The Blanc de Blancs, a subtle blending of 50 percent Ugni Blanc, 25 percent Rolle, 15 percent Grenache Blanc, and 10 percent Sauvignon Blanc, is a lively, fruity wine with good length and aromas of citrus, white-fleshed fruits, dried fruits, and spices— qualities that were rewarded by a Prix d'Excellence at a recent Vinalies competition, organized by the Union des Oenologues de France.

From Terres Blanches, there are two options for getting to Eygalières. You can either take the *route nationale* from Cavaillon, with its lovely plane trees, or the path leading from Terres Blanches. When you leave the hamlet of Destet, make a right in the direction of Maussane, where you cannot miss the hilltop Mas de Gourgonnier, whose windows all overlook the vines. The Cartier brothers' family has lived in this region for generations, and they can tell you all about it. This will be the last stage of your trip through the vineyards of the Baux de Provence, but not quite the end of your journey, for your voyage of initiation should be rounded off by a cool drink in the square of Maussane.

COTEAUX D'AIX-EN-PROVENCE:
WINES TO BE DRUNK YOUNG

Interspersed with patches of *garrigue* and woodland, the vineyards of the Coteaux d'Aix-en-Provence, the region that was such an inspiration to Cézanne, stretch all the way down to the shores of the Mediterranean. There is a taste for simplicity here, reflected in the unpretentious wines, wines that respect the sacrosanct trinity of sun, limestone, and the mistral.

Coteaux d'Aix is the second-largest appellation in southern France in terms of area, covering 10,000 acres (4,000 hectares), just behind the Côtes de Provence (36,750 acres [14,700 hectares]), but much larger than the third-placed Coteaux Varois (3,937 acres [1,575 hectares]). Its vineyards, 30 percent of which produce red wines, 65 percent rosés, and 5 percent whites, are located in the triangle of land between the Durance and the Mediterranean, stretching from the Rhône Valley to Mont Sainte-Victoire, and they include a small section of the Bouches-du-Rhône *département,* plus an enclave of two *communes* in the Var. The region is full of delightful tasting cellars that are well worth visiting. Once confined to this land of sunshades and shaded walks, the Coteaux d'Aix wines have acquired an excellent reputation. In a quest for quality, winemakers have been maturing their reds for longer to give them more depth and complexity, and many are suitable for laying down now. They have a deep ruby color and great structure, softer tannins, better balance, and mellower, more rounded flavors. The rosés, perfect for summer salads and barbecued meats, are a deep pink and are full and smooth in the mouth. The white wines are pale gold or greenish-gold in color and are bursting with tasty, refreshing fruitiness.

The history of the Coteaux d'Aix vineyards is bound up with the history of Provence. The Greeks arrived on the southern shores of France in the sixth century B.C. from what is now the Gulf of Smyrna. They founded Massilia, the old name for Marseille. In their luggage they brought with them such vine varieties as Ugni Blanc, which they planted on the surrounding hills. The Romans, those indefatigable conquerors, followed later, extending the plantings inland. In the fifteenth century A.D., René of Anjou, count of Provence, nicknamed "the winemaker king," made the region's wines famous throughout most of Europe. In his honor, in 1946, the wines of the Aix region became known as Coteaux du Roy René. Ten years later they were accorded status as a Vin Délimité de Qualité Supérieure and renamed Coteaux d'Aix, and in 1985, winemakers' efforts to improve quality were rewarded by the creation of the Appellation d'Origine Contrôlée Coteaux d'Aix-en-Provence.

ITINERARY

Château de Fonscolombe, one of the leading Provençal estates, is situated in the north of the appellation, in the picturesque village of Puy-Sainte-Réparade, in the heart of the Durance valley. Fonscolombe was built in 1720 by an ancestor of the present owners. It is a well-maintained château whose architecture displays an Italian Quattrocento influence. Vines were cultivated on this site from the time of Roman colonization, and by 1700, there were some large plots of vines on the property. The 160 acres (64 hectares) of vineyard abut the northern slopes of the Trévaresse range of hills. Their location opposite the Lubéron mountain range means that the vines come into leaf two weeks later than they do in the southern, coastal area of the appellation. The wines of Château de Fonscolombe are fruity and very drinkable, but should be drunk in their sprightly youth. The balanced reds, with their soft tannins, are aged in wood. They are a wonderful ruby color and are redolent of berries, making them an ideal accompaniment to barbecued meats, gratins, and broiled foods. Be sure to serve them slightly chilled, at between 57°F

WITH ITS AIR OF A TUSCAN COUNTRY HOUSE, THE EIGHTEENTH-CENTURY CHÂTEAU DE FONSCOLOMBE
IS FAMOUS FOR ITS METICULOUSLY MADE WINES THAT ARE FRAGRANT WITH THE PERFUME OF WHITE FLOWERS AND CITRUS,
AS EXEMPLIFIED BY ITS CUVÉE GOURMANDE, WHICH SHOULD BE DRUNK YOUNG.

and 59°F (14°C to 18°C). The whites are rich and generous, ideal as an aperitif or as an accompaniment to smoked salmon or grilled fish. The pride of the house is the Cuvée Spéciale. At its finest, this magnificent garnet-red wine has a bouquet of berries and spices. In the mouth it is supple and balanced, with tannins that are still young, a sign that it will age well. This fine wine can best be appreciated with *bœuf en croûte de sel*, red meat, or a selection of farmhouse cheeses.

Peter Fischer is an extraordinary character. He was born in Germany, the heir to the Uhu glue fortune. At an age when many boys want to grow up to be policemen, he was determined to be a winemaker and went on to study winemaking in California. As soon as he saw Revelette estate on the northern slopes of the famous Mont Sainte-Victoire, he fell in love with it. This is the northernmost winery in the appellation. Surrounded by forests, the sixty acres (twenty-four hectares) of vineyards are located near the little village of Jouques, which is famous for its climate, the coolest in the whole of Provence. In his approach to winemaking, Fischer's overriding aim is to preserve the natural balance. As a result, these are authentic Provençal wines, genuine products of the soil that are produced

organically. Fischer has refused to compromise and is critical of new technology. This meticulous winemaker relies on his instinct, refusing to irrigate and working his land in the old-fashioned way, without pesticides or fertilizers. His basic wines are typical of the district and good representatives of the appellation. They are pure and authentic, made entirely without "corrective" enological products, and should be drunk young. The white goes well with shellfish, the rosé makes a great aperitif and accompaniment to appetizers, and the red is a wonderful partner for grilled meats and leg of lamb. As for his top range of wines, these are a testament to the talent and creativity of this winemaker. Everything has been done to produce a rich, complex wine that is suitable for aging, as demonstrated by his Grand Rouge. This has a nose of rare finesse and an intense flavor that will enhance red meats and game. His white Bouches-du-Rhône *vin de pays*, known as the Grand Blanc de Revelette, is made entirely from Chardonnay grapes, partially aged in barrels for nine months and partially in vats. It goes wonderfully well with white meat and shellfish.

At the crossroads between Aix-en-Provence, the Lubéron, and the Alpilles, just a few rows of vines away from the great highway traveled by vacationers to the South of France, the Château Bas stands on a hill.

From here you can see as far as Lauris, Cavaillon, Mont Sainte-Victoire, and Étang de Berre. The only blot on this wonderful landscape is the viaduct built to carry the TGV Méditerranée high-speed train, which has disfigured the view looking toward the Lubéron. The château, built on the site of a Gallo-Roman citadel and restored in the seventeenth century, is a charming combination of rusticity and elegance. The farm, *chais*, and residence were all built at different periods, but combine gracefully without ever getting in each other's way. The wine presses, barrels, ancient olive trees, sheepfolds, and stables all testify to the agricultural heritage of this place dating back to the fifth century, and vines have been grown here since antiquity. Today, the estate's wines, made in all three colors, encapsulate the philosophy and expertise of the house. The red from the Pierres du Sud range is a blend of Cabernet Sauvignon, Syrah, and Grenache. Low yields have resulted in a full-bodied wine that has finesse and elegance. Dark in color, it has a rich, complex nose of cocoa and roasted coffee beans, which after aging develop into aromas of leather and plum. The Cuvée du Temple range contains the estate's top wines and features a rosé, an elegant white, and a rich, aromatic red wine made with grapes from the best plots. The wines of Château Bas are the stars of the appellation.

THE VINEYARD OF THE COTEAUX D'AIX, AT THE FOOT OF THE FAMOUS MONT SAINTE-VICTOIRE. THE LEGENDARY CHÂTEAU SIMONE (PRECEDING PAGE) MAKES SOME OF THE MOST CELEBRATED WINES IN THE SOUTH OF FRANCE. POPULAR WITH WINSTON CHURCHILL AND HERBERT VON KARAJAN AMONG OTHERS, THEY ARE THE JEWELS IN THE CROWN OF THE TINY APPELLATION OF PALETTE NEAR AIX-EN-PROVENCE, WHICH CONTAINS ONLY TWO WINEMAKERS. THE RED IS A DISTINGUISHED, VELVETY, FULL-BODIED WINE. THE WHITE IS GOLDEN IN COLOR DEEPENING WITH AGE AND HAS A RARE ELEGANCE AND COMPLEXITY.

CÔTES-DE-PROVENCE:
BETWEEN SEA AND MOUNTAIN

In this region suffocated by the pressures of the property market and tourism, it is a rare pleasure to be able to contemplate a hillside covered in a sea of vines. Here, green meets blue and the air is filled with the heady fragrances of the *garrigue* and pines. Fresh air at last!

While a number of vineyards occupy some of the most coveted land in Europe, close to sandy beaches and riverbanks, others can be found in more rugged country, on the slopes of Mont Sainte-Victoire, crisscrossed by the paths so beloved of the French writer Jean Giono. Unfortunately, small family-owned estates handed down from one generation to the next are becoming a rarity. The proximity of the Côte d'Azur, picture-postcard landscapes, and the sunny promise of eternal summer have attracted investors seeking to buy a lifestyle along with a vineyard. These new winemakers, most of them foreigners with inexhaustible stock options, have found ways, with commendable thoroughness and professionalism, of making hectares and hectares of vines profitable, producing very marketable wines that put the emphasis on quality. These magnificent vineyards have emerged from anonymity and are now producing wines with considerable added value—for those wine lovers who are not deterred by the price, of course.

The Côtes-de-Provence appellation was created in 1977 and today covers a territory of more than 52,500 acres (20,000 hectares) producing as many as 120 million bottles of red, white, and rosé wines a year. Rosé alone accounts for 81 percent of the appellations's production, 80 percent of which is planted in the Var *département*. The Bouches-du-Rhône is home to the Côtes de Provence de la Sainte-Victoire appellation, which covers an area of 5,000 acres (2,000 hectares), with an islet of twelve acres (five hectares) inside the Alpes-Maritimes at the village of Villars-sur-Var, behind Nice. The region is vast and diverse, but for the purposes of discussion can be broadly divided into three areas defined by their specific geological and climatic features.

The district traditionally known as the Hautes Côtes contains more than one third of the Côtes de Provence of the Var. Rubbing shoulders with the *garrigue* and the umbrella pines, the vines grow in soil colored pink madder by iron oxides. The climate here is affected by the proximity of the Alps. This part of Provence remains little known, hidden behind its truffle oaks and old drystone chapels.

Around the Gulf of Saint-Tropez, vine-growing continues today despite the temptations of property development. Vines cascade across the hillsides around Plan-de-la-Tour, Grimaud, Cogolin, and Ramatuelle, descending right to the tip of the peninsula. Further east, around Fréjus, they cover the slopes and parts of the plain between the Massif de l'Estérel and the Massif des Maures, sprouting out of the beautiful red earth. Vines were planted here by the Romans more than twenty centuries ago, and today they fight for space with heather, cork oaks, and umbrella pines. Between Saint-Tropez and Hyères to the west, the Massif des Maures rise out of the sea, offering the vines one of the most beautiful natural sites on the coast. Here the vines occupy parts of the highly protected coastline, rubbing shoulders with palm trees, golden mimosas, and flowering bay trees. Out to sea, the little-known *parc naturel régional* of the Island of Porquerolles protects the loveliest island vineyard of France. The grapes grow behind the wild beaches and picture-postcard villages to offer wines under the pretty name of Côtes-de-Provence des Îles.

It is hardly surprising, given such diversity of sites, that a multitude of grape varieties are used. The reds and rosés are made from Grenache, Syrah, Cinsaut, Mourvèdre, Cabernet Sauvignon, and Counoise. The native variety Tibouren is used for the elegant rosés, which have delicate, fruity aromas sometimes reminiscent of peaches.

THE VIEW FROM CLOS MIREILLE IS BREATHTAKING. THIS PROPERTY FACING THE HYÈRES ISLANDS
ONLY MAKES TWO WHITE WINES, A BLANC DE CÔTE AND A BLANC DE BLANCS.

As for the whites, Rolle, Ugni Blanc, Clairette, Grenache Blanc, Bourboulenc, and Sémillon are used to create blended wines that do not tolerate mediocrity. In the South of France making white wines that are not too heavy or alcoholic remains a difficult challenge.

The Côtes-de-Provence appellation is traditionally famous for its summer rosés, with their diaphanous, rose-petal colors and lively, aromatic, fruity flavors. However, there are also great red and white wines, as demonstrated by the *crus classés*. The story of these wines can be traced back to 1895, when a group of winemakers in the Var joined forces to defend and promote their wines. Their efforts led, in 1947, to the selection by a special commission of twenty-three estates based on a study of their *terroir*, expertise, and reputation. In July 1955, a ministerial decree gave these estates the prestigious title of *cru classé*, as used in the famous 1855 classification of wines in the Médoc and Sauternes. Of the 196 estates in France that can claim this distinction, fourteen are in Provence.

ITINERARY

Château Sainte-Roseline is one of the most visited estates in the Var. Its popularity is due to the fact that it is both a *cru classé* and a tourist attraction, thanks to its little chapel that houses the remains, in a glass coffin, of the only female saint in the *département*. Adorned with mosaics by Marc Chagall and a bas-relief by Diego Giacometti, the chapel stands next to the ambulatory of the convent, whose foundations date back to the eleventh century. Once dedicated to meditation, it is now a monument to modernity, thanks to the refurbishment of the interior by architect Jean-Michel Wilmotte. In 1993, when Françoise and Bernard Teillaud purchased Château Sainte-Roseline, where vines have been grown since the nineteenth century, the ruined convent had lost its splendor. Given carte blanche by the owner, Wilmotte decided to remove everything except but the walls, completely redesigning the interior spaces around the cloister. In order to accentuate the monastic character of the convent, he created a series of huge white rooms, whose ogival windows open onto the cloister and the luxuriant beds of lavender, rambling roses, and fragrant wisteria. The estate has 235 acres (95 hectares) of vines and makes wines in all three colors in a state-of-the-art three-story building. Owner Bernard Teillaud decided to put the emphasis on quality and reduced the proportion of rosés accordingly. They now represent only 50 percent of production, as compared with 90 percent for the rest of the appellation. The reds, which are sold at prices well above the average for the appellation, are intended for aging. In order to promote his wines, Teillaud has turned his estate into something of a cultural center, where concerts, plays, exhibitions, and themed events are organized. As a result, over the past nine years income from the property has multiplied nine-fold. The Prieuré range, the château's leading wines, are the result of

THE CHATEAU SAINT-MARTIN IS OWNED BY WOMEN WHO DISTILL LIQUID ELEGANCE IN ALL THREE COLORS, IN HOMAGE TO THE FORMER OWNERS OF THE FIRM (FACING PAGE). THE CHATEAU BELLET (BELOW), LOCATED EAST OF NICE, BEARS THE NAME OF ONE OF THE SMALLEST APPELLATIONS IN FRANCE. ITS RED WINES ARE FULL-BODIED, THE WHITES AROMATIC, AND THE ROSÉS EMINENTLY DRINKABLE.

low yields using grapes taken from the best plots. Particularly irresistible is the white, which is aged for a long time in barrels, emerging as a fine, perfumed, velvety wine, with delicious odors of vanilla, white peach, and pear. In short, a mystical wine.

On leaving the parking lot, take the first road on the right, a delightful country road that winds for miles, and eventually you will reach Château Font du Broc. Built in the style of a Mexican hacienda, this lavish, recently built property with its bright red ocher walls looks like a movie set. The wines are matured in a delightful Provençal-style edifice, with a cellar seventy feet (twenty meters) below ground whose ceiling is supported by a forest of vaults, arches, and pillars sculpted with grape leaves and bunches of grapes. The estate belongs to an industrialist from Marseille who owns a tire factory. It covers an area of 250 acres (100 hectares), surrounded by drystone walls and dotted with cypress and olive trees. Not surprisingly, similar care and thought have been lavished on the wines. The yields are very low, the grapes are picked by hand in the course of several pickings, and the reds and whites are aged in oak barrels. Like everything else here, the wines are beyond reproach.

In 1994, fencing champion Philippe Riboud and his wife, who was from the Var, wanted to settle in the region, and came across the Domaine du Château Roubine. It was love at first sight. The property, whose name in Provençal means "stream," is situated between Lorgues and Draguignan, in a vast natural bowl surrounded by pines and oaks. The estate once belonged to the Knights Templar, who sold it to the Order of Knights of St. John of Jerusalem in the late eighteenth century. The French Revolution laid waste its 62,000 acres (25,000 hectares). It now consists of 260 acres (105 hectares), surrounded by olive trees and fields of lavender, of which 158 acres (64 hectares) are planted with appellation vines. For the champion

fencer, winner of six Olympic medals, wine and fencing have a great deal in common, starting with "a great French tradition, precision of movement, and true elegance." This *cru classé*, which has become one of the finest wine estates of the region, is expressed in a trio of wines in as many colors. The Cuvée Château Roubine red has fine tannins and spicy red-fruit aromas, while the Cuvée de Bargemon red is complex and elegant, a wine to accompany the finest food. The third range, the Cuvée Philippe Riboud, has a new label each year based on the theme of fencing and designed by an artist. Jivko and Novaro are just two of the artists who have contributed designs.

To reach the Château de Saint-Martin from Roubine, go back along the winding D562 to Lorgues, and then take the D10 to Taradeau. The Château de Saint-Martin is a former priory where the monks of Lérins made wine until the eighteenth century. Since 1750, it has been run by the same illustrious family. This very selective *cru classé* has mainly been the work of the women of the family down the years. One of the most important was Adeline de Barry, who did much to develop the estate, which is only half an hour from Saint-Tropez and the same distance from the famous Gorges du Verdon. Before her, Marie-Anne, an enthusiastic botanist, laid out an informal garden in the English style that visitors can still admire. She was also responsible for building the château. She was followed by Louise Charlotte, who came by ship from Santo Domingo to get married here, with nothing but a closet to contain her trousseau for luggage. Then there was Louise Françoise Marie, whose tragic death led her father to erect a statue of the Virgin in her image. The statue stands on the hill, overlooking the cellar, as if watching over the wines. Yet despite this very feminine world, the estate was then owned by Count Rohan-Chabot. The count had a passion for women and fast cars and had the exciting idea of combining his two

THE CUVÉE CLARENDON MADE AT DOMAINE GAVOTY
(LEFT) IS NAMED FOR BERNARD GAVOTY, THE MUSIC CRITIC
OF THE NEWSPAPER LE FIGARO, WHOSE PENNAME IT WAS.
THE WINE IS HARMONIOUS AND OPULENT.
CHÂTEAU SAINTE ROSELINE (FACING PAGE) IS LOCATED
IN ONE OF THE OLDEST ABBEYS OF THE REGION, NEXT TO
THE CHAPEL IN WHICH THE ONLY SAINT OF THE VAR
DÉPARTEMENT IS BURIED.

interests by inaugurating the first automobile rally for women drivers, the Paris–Saint-Raphaël, a classic in its day. His daughter, Thérèse de Gasquet, is the current owner. A lover of history and tradition, she has allowed an archeological dig on her property to search for Gallo-Roman remains and staged a son et lumière show in the historic cellars of the château, a true sanctuary where wines have matured for centuries. In 2002, in homage to all the outstanding women who have run Château de Saint-Martin for 265 years, Adeline created a series of wines in their image, the Comtesse range. It contains red, white, and rosé wines, each produced using grapes from old vines, and each displaying as much personality as the women who inspired them. Particularly fine is the salmon-pink rosé, a wine which on no account should be drowned in ice cubes. With its nose of quince, this rosé is as balanced, elegant, and as carefully nurtured as a *grand cru. Noblesse oblige!*

From Las Vegas to New York via Cannes, there's hardly a single prestigious restaurant whose wine list does not include something from the Domaines d'Ott. World famous for its rosés, especially the Cœur de Grain, this illustrious firm has many loyal customers. Its Blanc de Blancs, now fifty years old, was the favorite of French artist and playwright Jean Cocteau, who introduced all his friends to it.

It was in 1936 that Marcel Ott, a stubborn Alsatian, bought Clos Mireille, which he had run hitherto as a tenant farmer. He decided to create a great rosé wine and replant the estate with noble varieties. This is how the Cœur de Grain was born, a wine considered by many experts to be the finest rosé in the world. After completely replanting the vineyard, Marcel Ott decided to market his wines himself. Aware that much of his clientele lived on the French Riviera, he opened a wine store in Antibes. The business passed from father to son and one of his descendants, René Ott, was responsible for the famous bottle shape that since the 1930s has been photographed with some of the biggest stars in the world. Although Clos Mireille now only makes white wines, there is a little wine museum in a corner of the cellar that traces the whole story.

The lands of Clos Mireille surround a handsome eighteenth-century Provençal mansion (*bastide*) and run right down to the sea. In this dream landscape, the vines run parallel to a beach caressed by sea breezes and are surrounded by pine trees. For those whose only experience of this coast are the large seaside resorts with their incessant traffic jams and overcrowded beaches, this place evokes a forgotten coastline of stunning beauty, facing the islands of Hyères on the horizon. Benefiting from the cool sea spray, the terrain is suitable for producing exceptional white wines from Sémillon, which contributes suppleness and roundness, and Ugni Blanc, which gives them youth and vigor. Of Clos Mireille's 420 acres (170 hectares), only 116 acres (47 hectares) are used for vine-growing and only white varieties are cultivated. Based on the axiom that whatever is added to the land or the wine will eventually wind up in the body of the taster, the only fertilizer used is organic. The vines are espaliered on wires and the wines are aged in oak.

Tasting these wines, it is impossible not to fall under the spell of the Blanc de Blancs, with its nutty, spicy aromas mingled with those of wild flowers, or the Blanc de Côte, whose devotees drink it right through a meal, from the aperitif to the goat cheese. It is particularly refreshing for a wine from this region. As for the prestigious and confidential Insolent, which is not available for tasting because it is produced in such small quantities, the purchase of a bottle will be a rare treat for a special occasion and a delicious gift to those one holds dearest.

Upon leaving the estate, make a left along a little country road that leads to Clos Mireille's nearest neighbor, the Château de Léoubes. This huge estate, covering 1,482 acres (600 hectares), was bought in 1997 by a British industrialist. Today, 124 acres (fifty hectares) of vines and thirty acres (twelve hectares) of olive trees are under cultivation. The undergrowth gradually gives way to serried ranks of vines and the area has been landscaped to look most attractive. The estate includes two miles of coastline facing the islands of Hyères, and two creeks from the Fort de Brégançon run through it. Here you can find a pristine Provence, wild and appealing. In addition to wine, olive oil is produced here, sold in attractive bottles that would grace the finest dining table. The fresh, aromatic rosé has a nose that conjures up the fruits of the sun. In the mouth it has a supple, ample attack of great finesse and a long finish. In short, what appears to be a simple summer wine turns out to have astonishing complexity.

THE CELLAR AT CHÂTEAU SAINTE-ROSELINE,
REDESIGNED BY ARCHITECT JEAN-MICHEL WILMOTTE,
RESEMBLES A LIBRARY IN WHICH THE WONDERFUL
WINES OF THE HOUSE ARE CAREFULLY ARRANGED,
SOME OF THEM BOTTLED IN THE UNUSUAL
LAMPE DE MÉDUSE BOTTLE WITH ITS BULGING BASE.

CORSICA: SUBLIME MUSCATS,
FRAGRANT REDS, AND AROMATIC WHITES

Corsica is not an island, it's a mountain in the sea. The terrain rises to a height of over two thousand meters (seven thousand feet) and plunges steeply into the sea. As a result, the vines extend their foliage toward the mountain while their feet are almost under water.

From the creeks linked with pine forests around Porto Vecchio to the cliffs of Bonifacio, from the desert of Agriates to the rocky inlets of Piana, via the golden sands of Campomoro Bay, Corsica is full of contrasts and extremes. Its rugged, wild valleys all benefit from the mild Mediterranean climate and a special exposure and microclimate that are particularly beneficial for vines. There are four main soil types: granite on the west side; schist in the north, including Cap Corse; chalk and clay in Patrimonio and to the south of it; alluvial and marly sand from Solenzara to Bastia on the east coast. There are more than thirty native varieties of grape, including the "holy trinity"—Sciacarello, Nielluccio, and Vermentino—which can be found in all the appellations. Corsica's disparate characteristics, an integral part of its identity, are the reason for the island's nine Appellations d'Origine Contrôlée.

Corsica gets six times less rain than the Bordeaux region in August and September and six hundred hours more sun. Although still relatively little known, Corsican wines have improved greatly in recent years. Their aromas are redolent of the *maquis*, spices, and berries. They are high in tannins and, just like the Corsicans themselves, full of character. In short, these are wines that are just waiting to be discovered.

The appellations cover an area of 6,830 acres (2,732 hectares), the total area planted with vines being more than 17,000 acres (6,800 hectares). There are 188 producers in all, including ninety private wineries and six cooperatives. Red wines account for 45 percent of the island's production, rosés for a slightly smaller percentage, and white wines for 20 percent. Corsican wines must contain at least 50 percent of the traditional native varieties: Nielluccio, Sciacarello, and Vermentino.

Nielluccio, the most popular and widely grown of the Corsican varieties, was introduced by the Pisans in the twelfth century. This is this grape that has given the wines of the Patrimonio region their high reputation. Nielluccio seems to encapsulate the complexity of the *maquis*. Wines made from it have a nose of hare fur and licorice, berries and apricots, with an occasional surprise in the form of spices and violets. They are dark, almost black in color and high in alcohol. In some appellations Nielluccio may be blended with a little Syrah. Unblended and aged for a long time, it produces a robust wine with a bouquet of wild plants.

Sciacarello is the most native of all the varieties and grows best on granitic soil. Its hallmarks are freshness, finesse, and a peppery aroma. The juicy grapes prosper along the coast west of Ajaccio. They produce a wine with a lovely garnet color, with fine, silky tannins and enough acidity to be suitable for laying down.

Vermentino, also known as Malvoisie, is the star of the island's white varieties. It expresses subtle notes of hawthorn, almond, and apple, giving real personality to white wines. When combined with red varieties, it produces rounded, attractive rosés. When grown in granitic soil, it can bring liveliness to a wine; in chalk and clay, the results are smoother. The wines made from it are dry and balanced, and their appearance varies from diaphanous to golden.

Petitgrain Muscat, the last of the native varieties, has been grown around Cap Corse from time immemorial. Far from resulting in syrupy or sugary wines, it has a nose reminiscent of floral perfumes and honey, allied with remarkable freshness.

In 35 B.C., the Roman poet Virgil extolled the virtues of the wine of Balagne. Greeks from Phocaea planted the first vines, but

CORSICA HAS NINE APPELLATIONS PRODUCING REDS,
WHITES, AND ROSÉS THAT ARE AS STRONG IN CHARACTER
AS THE LOCAL INHABITANTS.

it was the Genoese, who ruled the island from the late thirteenth century until 1769, who were responsible for greatly expanding vine growing. By the nineteenth century, almost every village was making its own wines from trellised vines. Then along came the phylloxera aphid and destroyed 85 percent of the grape vines. The two World Wars, followed by a massive migration from the countryside, delayed the replanting of vines in the twentieth century. In the early 1960s, Corsica was settled by a wave of former French inhabitants of North Africa, and the east coast of the island began to be planted with high-yielding varieties such as Aramon, Alicante, and Carignan. Twenty years later, a new approach led to the restructuring of Corsican vineyards, with greater emphasis on quality. Some 50,000 acres (20,000 hectares) of vines disappeared and traditional varieties better suited to local conditions were planted. These changes laid the foundations for the island's nine appellations: Patrimonio, Ajaccio, Coteaux du Cap Corse, Muscat du Cap Corse, Calvi, Sartène, Figari, Porto Vecchio, and Corse.

As soon as you cross the Col de Teghime just west of Bastia, a vast panorama opens up with the sea in the distance and, in the middleground, the rocks that surround the island's most famous vineyard. This magic triangle between Saint-Florent, Murato, and Patrimonio, at the bottom end of Cap Corse, is where the first Corsican Appellation d'Origine Contrôlée was born in 1968. The Patrimonio appellation is sheltered from frost and harsh winds and consists of fragmented plots, clearings in the surrounding scrubland that cover a huge natural arena surrounded by hills. The soil consists of shale covered by a thin layer of chalk and it is here that Nielluccio gives of its best. In terms of soil, the Nebbio region that is home to the Patrimonio appellation is a sort of island within an island and its geology is undoubtedly a key factor in the wine's quality. Long considered as a wine to be drunk as soon as it has been made, red Patrimonio is now also a wine for keeping. White Patrimonio is made from the Vermentino variety, which is harvested late and is similar to Muscat.

Although Cap Corse lies only a few vine plants north of Patrimonio, this finger pointing toward continental Europe has something of Ireland about it due to its windswept landscape. On the coast, the well-tended properties are indicators of the prosperity that came from a wine that was once exported to countries as distant as Venezuela. Today, the Cap Corse appellation, produced by four winemakers from seventy-two acres (thirty-three hectares), contains reds suitable for aging and sought-after, elegant whites

THE PATRIMONIO APPELLATION IS A WONDERFUL
LANDSCAPE THAT TAKES IN THE SEA AND THE VINEYARD.
TWO LOCAL GRAPE VARIETIES—NIELLUCCIU AND SCIACARELLO—
ARE USED HERE, PRODUCING WINES WITH GOOD AGING POTENTIAL.

with pronounced floral aromas. La Balagne, whose 723 acres (293 hectares) of vines lie between Calvi and L'Ile-Rousse, looks like a beautiful garden, nestling in a natural amphitheater with a sea view. This is a landscape of olive trees, wheat fields, sheep, orchards, and umbrella pines that has an air of Tuscany about it. Now the Corse Calvi appellation, this is an ancient wine-growing region, and the richest on the island. Its wines are straightforward and unpretentious, but with a rebellious streak that gives them a particular charm. Here the narrow roads pass drystone buildings and terraced vines. This is where Sciacarello was first planted, and the variety gives this wine of the hills its clearly identifiable aromas of almond and black currant.

The 557 acres (223 hectares) of the Ajaccio appellation are planted mainly with red varieties and the powerful wines are recognizable by their slight odor of gunflint due to the granitic soil on which the vines are grown. The rosés are full of finesse and the whites are very floral. The plantings of the Golfe de Sartène cover 450 acres (180 hectares) and are made up of the most authentic Corsican varieties, giving rise to opulent, powerful red wines. The whites are shot with jade and are full and fresh, and even the attractive rosés have body. It is said that Napoleon had a weakness for these brightly colored, robust wines.

In the far south of the island, some seventy-five acres (thirty-four hectares) of vines grow at the foot of the jagged peak of the Omu di Cagna, in beautiful, lustrous soil concealed behind a row of parasol pines standing stiffly to attention. The wines produced here have surprising finesse, making the Corse Figari appellation one of the most promising on the island. The arid, windswept region that sweeps down to the sea here is reached by heading southwest from Porto Vecchio. Its red soil brings to mind the hills of the Massif de l'Estérel on the Côte d'Azur. Here, however, it forms a plain that offers nothing to lovers of the picturesque. The 165 acres (sixty-six hectares) of the Corse Porto Vecchio appellation produce round, elegant red wines, fine and aromatic rosés, and dry, fruity white wines that are the delight of seafood lovers.

Between Porto Vecchio and Bastia stretches a vast plain abutting an endless line of rocky mountain crags that spin away into the distance. The 3,215 acres (1,286 hectares) of vines form the largest grape-producing region of the island. The wines made here—reds, whites, and rosés—form the bulk of the Vins de Corse appellation, honest wines with rustic charm.

ITINERARY

The current owner of Domaine Orenga de Gaffory on Cap Corse, Henri Orenga de Gaffory, is the great-grandson of the founder of the firm, Louis Napoléon Mattei. He became a winemaker after starting out in sparkling mineral water, because one of the subsidiaries of the family firm is the concession for Orezza spring water. Henri worked there until the firm was left to him in the 1970s and he decided to move to Patrimonio, where his father had planted vines. Having trained on the fifty-seven acres (twenty-three hectares) of his father's vineyard, Henri now directs operations like an orchestral conductor, single-handedly managing the exploitation of the different plots and fixing harvest dates in order to get the best out of them. "Everything happens there, begins there. It is the vine that calls the shots. You can have the best enologist in the world working for you, but it's pointless unless you have quality grapes." He lists the finer points of the Nielluccio variety that is used in his *cuvées*, each of which has a distinctive character according to how it is vinified and aged. The clayey, chalky soil enables the roots to grow deep and the grapes to ripen even during a drought. His palette of wines includes a Muscat that has become a classic of its kind, appearing on the wine lists of the finest restaurants, as well as a rosé that is deep salmon-pink color and is fruity and smooth in the mouth with a pleasing acidity.

If wine is Henri Orenga de Gaffory's first love, his second is contemporary art. He was initiated at a very young age and started his modern art collection around fifteen years ago. He now has approximately one hundred works stored in his wine cellar. He strongly believes that the appreciation of both art and wine is a matter of perception, of sensual pleasure, so in 1991 he organized the first art exhibition in his wine cellar. Since then, he has been hosting contemporary painters, sculptors, photographers, and other artists, local and foreign, combining good food and culture. Who says culture never fed anyone?

Clos Capitoro, with its famous bull's head logo, is twelve kilometers east of Ajaccio, just off the N196 on the little road to Pisciatella, which winds gently through a wild landscape. The building dates from 1856 and is divided into five sections. The feeling of venerable age is enhanced by the heavy, solid, chestnut-wood doors. The old stone walls are covered with Virginia creeper, contrasting attractively with the bright red shutters. Opposite is the equally charming family home that occupies a former post-house. Jacques, the current owner, is also the mayor of this little village. Clos Capitoro, the leading winery in the Ajaccio appellation, has belonged to the Bianchetti family for several generations. It enjoys a high reputation outside Corsica because it is one of the seven Corsican estates honored with three stars in Robert Parker's *Wine Buyer's Guide*. The vineyards cover 124 acres (fifty hectares) divided into three plots, Punta di Cuccu (thirty-seven acres [fifteen hectares]), Paviglia (fifty acres [twenty hectares]), and Capitoro (thirty-seven acres [fifteen hectares]). The terrain here is made up of granitic slopes and clay and silica soil. Traditional cultivation techniques are used—plowing, harrowing, hoeing, and harvesting are all performed manually, and no weed killers are used. As well as appellation wines, the winery also produces *vins doux naturels*, as well as a sparkling *blanc de blancs* called the Impérial Cyrnos, made using the *méthode champenoise* and the only sparkling wine of its type on the island. The red is a light ruby in color, with a pronounced nose of pepper, spices, and sour cherries. It combines the velvety smoothness and high alcoholic content of Grenache with the delicate tannins of Sciacarello, which has a slightly woody flavor despite being aged in a vat rather

The Muscat Blanc à Petits Grains variety (facing page) has provided Corsica with vins doux naturels that can be more subtle than those of the mainland. Each wine is a work of art at the Clos Canarelli in Figari (right), which is run by one of the most promising winemakers on the island.

than in wood. These reds are a perfect match for red meats and game, and should be drunk at around 63°F to 64°F (17°C to 18°C). In the case of the two *vins doux naturels*, the first is based on Grenache and is a Banyuls-type wine that should be drunk at 59°F (15°C) as a superb accompaniment to any type of dessert. The second is made using over-ripe Vermentino grapes and is a delightful aperitif. As for the rosé, it remains lively for the first ten months after vinification and should be drunk young. Salmon-pink in color, it has a fruity nose and a lively, balanced feel in the mouth. It is the archetypal well-made thirst-quencher. The *blanc de blancs*, which is made by following the complex stages of the *méthode champenoise*, uses the Vermentino variety.

The Domaine Pietri de Saparale was once the pride of Sartène. It comprises 250 acres (100 hectares) of vines, imposing *chais*, and a majestic manor house with a belltower whose bell is used to summon the employees, as well as workers' cottages and a chapel where the vine

and God may come together. The fragrance of mint escapes from the ancient fieldstone, shaded by an ancient magnolia tree. Young wine-maker Philippe Farinelli has installed his wine cellar in part of the old buildings in a bid to restore this prestigious estate to its former glory.

The Clos d'Alzeto, the highest winery on the island, is one of the jewels of the Ajaccio appellation. It is situated at an altitude of between 400 and 500 meters overlooking the Golfe de la Liscia, surrounded by magnificent scenery. The vineyards face southwest, occupying the slopes of the valley of the Cinarca. Protected from salty sea breezes, the vines enjoy excellent climatic conditions despite the altitude, with cool nights and warm days. The estate covers an area of 105 acres (42 hectares) and has belonged to the same family since 1820. Pascal Albertini is continuing the tradition, combining age-old know-how, modernity, and respect for nature with a single objective—a quest for the finest quality. Here, the grapes are picked by

hand and the harvest is delayed as long as possible. This respect for ancestral methods is combined with the latest techniques in order to ensure perfect vinification. The vats have automatic raising of the must and are programmable for optimum extraction of colors and tannins. Fermentation is temperature-controlled and reduced-pressure bottling is used. The Prestige red is a blend of Sciacarello and Nielluccio. Vinification extracts the best of the tannins and these are refined by maturing, giving the whole blend power and finesse. The Tradition red, which is a strong wine, consists mainly of Sciacarello, the leading variety of the appellation, blended with Grenache and Nielluccio. Maturing in the cellar improves the bouquet and refines the tannins. The rosé, made predominantly from Sciacarello, is distinguished by its finesse and fruitiness in the nose as well as in the mouth. It is pale in appearance, has a delicate, fruity nose, and a smooth feel with slight acidity and good length on the palate.

IN LUMIO, ABOVE CALVI, THE VINEYARDS ARE PLANTED ON SHALE. THE PROXIMITY OF THE SEA AND THE ALTITUDE OF THE VINEYARD RESULT IN INTENSE, POWERFUL, AND GENEROUS WINES.

USEFUL ADDRESSES

THE SOUTHWEST

CAHORS

INFORMATION
Office de Tourisme,
place François Mitterand,
Cahors.
Tel. 05 65 53 20 65.
www.tourisme-lot.com

**Comité Départemental
du Tourisme du Lot,**
107 quai Cavaignac, Cahors.
Tel. 05 65 35 07 09.

DISCOVER THE VINEYARDS
La Maison du Vin,
430 avenue Jean Jaurès,
46000 Cahors.
Tel. 05 65 23 22 24.
A free booklet entitled the *Livret du Vin de Cahors* is available (in French), listing two hundred local wineries that are open to the public.

ACCOMMODATION
Le Mas Azémar, rue du Mas de Vinssou, 46090 Mercuès.
Tel. 05 65 30 96 85.
Run by a former fashion photographer, this eighteenth-century house offers six spacious guest rooms, two of which would suit families. The homemade jams make breakfast here an unforgettable experience.

Hôtel Terminus,
5 avenue Charles Freycinet,
46000 Cahors.
Tel. 05 65 53 32 00.
Located opposite the station, this three-star hotel is both cozy and convivial, with first-rate service.

Château de Mercuès,
46090 Mercuès.
Tel. 05 65 20 00 01.
Overlooking the Lot valley, this château was formerly the summer residence of the bishops of Cahors. Now part of the Relais et Châteaux network, it offers breathtaking vistas and thirty superbly appointed guest rooms. Our favorite is located in the turret, with a bathroom on the floor below.

Domaine de Labarthe,
46090 Espère.
Tel. 05 65 30 92 34.
Three spacious and tastefully decorated guest rooms, furnished in a classical style with family heirlooms. Restful atmosphere, delightful hosts, and breakfast served in the charming kitchen.

Château de la Coste,
46700 Grézels.
Tel. 05 65 21 34 18.
Set amongst twenty-two acres (nine hectares) of vineyard overlooking the Lot valley, this former castle was refurbished during the Renaissance. It offers a suite and four guest rooms, all of which are beautifully appointed, and there is even a wine museum. Exquisite *table d'hôte* dining.

Hôtel Bellevue, place de la Mairie, 46700 Puy-L'Evêque.
Tel. 05 65 36 06 60.
Perched above the Lot valley, the views from this hotel are dizzying. Eleven airy rooms, decorated in a romantic, contemporary style, and a glass-walled restaurant that serves light and elegant gastronomic delights.

RESTAURANTS
Côté Lot,
place de la Truffière,
46700 Puy-L'Evêque.
Tel. 05 65 36 06 60.
A truly panoramic lookout over the twists and turns of the Lot valley. The style of decoration is as contemporary as the uplifting recipes, cooked to perfection by one of chef Jean-Marie Amat's acolytes.

Le Balandre,
5 avenue Charles de Freycinet,
Cahors.
Tel. 05 65 53 32 00.
This one-star restaurant performs gastronomic gymnastics with its new "modern light" slant on traditional regional fare. Wicked desserts.

WINES
Clos Triguedina,
46700 Puy-L'Evêque.
Tel. 05 65 21 30 81.
Owner: Jean-Luc Baldès.
The most talented winemaker of the appellation harvests his grapes by moonlight to ensure cool conditions. This helps to preserve aromas, as demonstrated by his Cuvée Prince Probus, with its powerful nose of spices and dark berries.

Château du Cayrou,
46700 Puy-L'Evêque.
Tel. 05 65 22 40 26.
Owners: Jouffreau family.
Two great châteaux run by two sisters. The wines of the Clos de Gamot are complex and powerful, and should not be drunk too soon. They are closed when young, but as they age they become more assured and fuller. Superb.

Château du Cèdre,
46700 Vire-sur-Lot.
Tel. 05 65 36 53 87.
Owners:
Pascal and Jean-Marc Verhaeghe-Bru. As the instigators of the Cahors wine quality charter, these winemakers are skilled, meticulous, and talented. Le Prestige offers roundness, powerfulness and elegance.

Château Lagrézette,
46140 Caillac.
Tel: 05 65 20 07 42.
Owner: Alain Dominique Perrin.
This château produces no fewer than twelve different wines vinified by Michel Rolland, including the fine Dame d'Honneur, made from the oldest vines on the estate, and Le Pigeonnier, a wine for laying down made entirely from the Auxerrois variety.

Château de Caix,
46140 Luzech.
Tel. 05 65 20 13 22.
This vineyard is owned by the Danish royal family and produces subtle red and white wines, including La Cigaralle du Château de Caix, a very fine white blended from Sémillon, Sauvignon, and Chardonnay grapes.

Château Pineraie,
46700 Puy-L'Evêque.
Tel. 05 65 30 82 07.
Owner: Burc et Fils Leygues.
The estate covers ninety-one acres (thirty-seven hectares) and contains all the soil types that are characteristic of the appellation. It's Cuvée Authentique, made mainly from old vines of

Auxerrois, combines finesse and strong character.

Château Lamartine,
46700 Soturac.
Tel. 05 65 36 54 14.
Fax: 05 65 24 65 31.
Owner: Alain Gayraud.
Strongly recommended are the velvety Cuvée Particulière, with its complex nose of blueberries and black currant, and the Expression, which has aromas of gingerbread and preserved fruits and smooth, soft tannins.

GAILLAC

INFORMATION
Office de Tourisme,
Abbaye Saint-Michel,
81600 Gaillac.
Tel. 05 63 57 61 37.
www.tourisme.fr
La Maison du Vin at the Abbaye Saint-Michel is *the* place to discover the full range of Gaillac wines. Its tasting facilities and sales outlet offer a one-stop introduction to all the region's wines. Tel. 05 63 57 15 40.
Tourisme et Vin arranges trips to meet winemakers and farm producers, as well as organizing on-site visits. Tel. 05 63 57 53 77.

ACCOMMODATION
Château de Mayragues,
81140 Castelnau de Montmirail.
Tel. 05 63 33 94 08.
Two guest rooms at one of the region's finest wine estates. With its hemp walls, exposed beams, sophisticated décor, and English-style breakfast, it has everything—even a great view.

Château de Salettes,
81140 Cahuzac sur Vère.
Tel. 05 63 33 60 63.
A three-star establishment where everything looks brand new and perfection rules, from the décor with its contemporary furniture to the view over the vineyards. The ideal setting for a weekend away for two.

Lucile Pinon, 8 place Saint-Michel, 81600 Gaillac.
Tel. 05 63 57 61 48.
Five guest rooms, two with views of the abbey and river Tarn, set on two floors. Breakfast is served on the terrace in summer against this breathtaking backdrop.

Château Larroze,
81140 Cahuzac sur Vère.
Tel. 05 63 33 99 70.
Owners:
Monsieur and Madame Noblet.
Located on a hillside, this small early nineteenth-century château overlooks the surrounding vineyards. Its two guest rooms—one of which is housed in a separate outbuilding—are spacious and finely appointed in muted tones.

RESTAURANTS
L'Epicurien,
Pelègre, 81600 Aussac.
Tel. 05 63 53 10 70.
Impeccable in terms of both food and atmosphere, this is an exceptional address that deserves to be kept a secret.
Reservations essential.

La Table du Sommelier,
34 place Thiers,
81000 Gaillac.
Tel. 05 63 81 20 10.
This chirpy bistro-boutique tucked beneath the arches offers cheap and cheerful dishes and wines, as well as a whimsical set menu to let you sample the delights of the traditional local fare.

Le Romuald,
6 rue du Port,
81310 Lisle sur Tarn.
Tel. 05 63 33 38 85.
A delightful half-timbered sixteenth-century house serving thick juicy steaks cooked over an open fire at prices that are easy on the pocket.

ACTIVITIES
Cave de Rabastens,
33 route d'Albi, 81800 Rabastens.
Tel. 05 63 33 73 80.
The winemakers here arrange a bus tour on the first Sunday of each summer month. Called Le Vin au Fil de l'Eau ("Wine along the Water"), it takes visitors through the history of the region from the Middle Ages to the present day, visiting vineyards, dovecotes, and the river. And it's free.

WINES
Domaine Vayssette,
route de Caussade,
81600 Gaillac.
Tel. 05 63 57 31 95.
Owners: Maryse, Jacques, and Patrice Vayssette.

This estate regularly wins medals. Particularly fine are the white dessert wines and Léa, a seductive, concentrated red.

Domaine des Très Cantous,
81140 Cahuzac sur Vère.
Tel. 05 63 33 90 40.
Owners: Bernard and Robert Plageoles.
The star of the appellation, producing wines that are true to the grape varieties. Everything is excellent here, but the Vin d'Autan stands out. It is a sweet dessert wine with a complex nose of peach, fig, banana, and apricot. Such quality comes at a price, of course.

Château de Mayragues,
81140 Castelnau de Montmirail.
Tel. 05 63 33 94 08.
Fax: 05 63 33 98 10.
www.chateau-de-mayragues.com
Owners: Laurence and Alan Geddes.
The Scottish owner of this château uses biodynamic methods. There is a small output of distinguished wines, including a red known as Clos des Mages, which has a delicious fragrance of raspberries and bell peppers, and a superb late-harvest wine that smells of Seville oranges, quince, and pineapple.

Domaine de Salettes,
81140 Cahuzac sur Vère.
Tel. 05 61 84 92 92.
Fax: 05 61 84 92 42.
Owner: Roger Lenet.
Reds and sweet and dry whites with lovely fragrances of eucalyptus and good complexity in the mouth. The wines are as worth exploring as the location.

Domaine de Causse Marine,
81140 Vieux.
Tel. 05 63 33 98 30.
Owner: Patrice Lescarret.
This original and brilliant ambassador for Gaillac surprises us with each wine. The white Les Greilles, the Duras Le Causse reds, the sweet wines Grain de Folie, and Délires d'Automne are all preeminent.

Château Clement Terme,
Les Fortis, 81310 Lisle sur Tarn.
Tel. 05 63 40 47 80.
Owner: Martine David.
Reds, dry whites, dessert wines,

slightly sparkling whites, and rosés—almost every type of wine is made here. You will get a warm welcome and the architecture is typical of the region.

Château de Saurs,
81310 Lisle sur Tarn.
Tel. 05 63 57 09 79.
Owner: Marie Paule Burrus Saurs.
The reds, whites, and rosés are as elegant and luscious as this château inhabited by a Swiss banker.

Domaine Rotier,
81600 Cadalen.
Tel. 05 63 41 75 14.
Owners:
Alain Rotier and Francis Marre.
The wonderful Renaissance has a nose of green apples and a lively flavor reminiscent of tropical fruits notably pineapple and lychee.

Domaine de Labarthe,
81150 Cestayrols.
Tel. 05 63 56 80 14.
Fax: 05 63 56 84 81.
This family has been making wine since 1550 on 120 acres (48 hectares) of vines planted around the property. The red Cuvée Guillaume and the sweet white Les Grains d'Or do not need their gold medals to convince of their quality.

Chateau Lastours,
81310 Lisle sur Tarn.
Tel. 05 63 57 07 09.
The white Cuvée Spéciale, with its aroma of dried fruits, is very good, while the Les Graviers is a very nice red.

MADIRAN/PACHERENC DU VIC-BILH

INFORMATION
Comité Départemental du Tourisme,
6 rue Eugène Ténot,
65000 Tarbes.
Tel. 05 62 56 48 00.

Office de Tourisme,
3 cours Gambetta,
65000 Tarbes.
Tel. 05 62 51 30 31.

La Maison des Vins de Madiran,
65700 Madiran.
Tel. 05 62 31 90 67.
www.vins-du-sud-ouest.com

ACCOMMODATION

Château de Sombrun,
65700 Sombrun.
Tel. 05 62 96 49 43.
At the end of a driveway lined with lime trees stands this eighteenth-century estate. Five delightful guest rooms with antique furniture. Swimming pool. Reservation required for dinner.

Château Montus,
65700 Castelnau Rivière-Basse.
Tel. 05 62 31 70 20.
The château of the appellation's leading property has ten comfortable guest rooms, surprising in their contemporary style of décor and bold colors, and a gourmet restaurant, open only from March to November.

Château du Bascou,
Lieu dit Saint-Go,
32290 Bouzon-Gellenave.
Tel. 05 62 69 04 12.
Three guest rooms, each named for one of the region's varieties of vine, in a character-filled house at the heart of the vineyards. Enjoy hearty Gascon cuisine and wines in the evening at the *table d'hôte* of this couple of hotelier-winegrowers.

RESTAURANTS

La Chaumière de Bidouze,
route de Saint-Mont,
32400 Riscle.
Tel. 05 62 69 86 56.
A farmhouse inn with a highly convivial atmosphere and its own *foie gras* cottage canning business. Fourteen attic rooms decorated with bric-a-brac gleaned from various places. The cuisine is not for light eaters.

Auberge la Bergeraye,
32110 Saint Martin d'Armagnac.
Tel. 05 62 09 08 72.
In this charming Bas Armagnac inn located between Riscle and Nogaro, none other than Pierrette Sarran—mother of the famous Toulouse chef Michel Sarran—tends the stove. Enough said.

Ferme Auberge du Madiranais,
Arroses, 64350 Lembeye.
Tel. 05 59 68 16 08.
A taste of the countryside, with regional cuisine at its best. On the menu: soup, *foie gras*, *poule au pot*, *magret*, cheese, and dessert.

EVENTS

The Fête des Vendanges is held in Crouseilles in mid-September, at the same time as the Automnales du Vic-Bilh.
"Portes ouvertes" in Madiran: on the last Sunday in November, château owners open the doors of their *chais* for wine tasting, sampling of local farmhouse foods, and other activities. Information: La Maison des Vins de Madiran, Tel. 05 62 31 90 67.

WINES

The best producers of Madiran are often also the best producers of Pacherenc.

Château Montus,
65700 Castelnau Rivière Basse.
Château Bouscassé,
32400 Maumusson.
Tel. 05 62 69 74 67.
Owner: Alain Brumont.
Often compared to their Médoc counterparts, the wines here are matured in oak barrels and are strong, aromatic, and powerful. The Vieilles Vignes and Prestige are wines for laying down, as are the Pacherenc wines Brumaire and Frimaire, which are on a par with Sauternes.

Domaine Berthoumieu,
32400 Viella.
Tel. 05 62 69 74 90.
Owner: Didier Barré-Dutour.
The Barré family have been winemakers since 1850 and they work their vineyard by hand. The yields are low and the grapes are picked by hand, resulting in exceptional wines such as the Haute Tradition, a favorite with many *sommeliers*, and the Charles de Batz, which is so concentrated that it needs decanting two hours before serving.

Château d'Aydie,
64330 Aydie.
Tel. 05 59 04 08 00.
Owners: Laplace family.
The Laplace family are members of the slow food movement and offer a workshop on their property during the grape harvest. The Château d'Aydie wine, made from 90 percent Tannat, is dark with a complex nose containing notes of vanilla and powerful but velvety tannins. In dry Pacherenc wines, the château produces a white with a nose of citrus and honey with a refreshing finish.

Cave de Crouseilles,
64350 Crouseilles.
Tel. 05 59 68 10 93.
This cooperative produces three Pacherencs each made from grapes harvested at a different time. For Folie du Roi, the grapes are harvested when only slightly overripe, during October; the Grain de Givre is made from the second sorting of grapes in late November; and for Hivernale the grapes are picked on December 21, the first day of the winter solstice. As for the red Madiran, the Prenium is a *vin de garde* which should be left in the cellar for at least ten years.

Château de Mascaraas,
Mascaraas-Haron, 64330 Garlin.
Tel. 05 59 04 92 60.
This private property is listed as a historic monument and has the finest decoration of any building in the northern Pyrénées-Atlantiques. It is open to the public with guided tours all year round. The winery produces a fine red Pacherenc with notes of black currant and spices, vinified by the Cave de Crouseilles.

CÔTES DE SAINT-MONT

INFORMATION

Syndicat d'Initiative,
6 place du Foirail, 32400 Riscle.
Tel. 05 62 69 74 01.

Office de Tourisme,
place du Général de Gaulle,
40800 Aire-sur-Adour.
Tel. 05 58 71 64 70.
www.aire-sur-adour.org
"Routes des Vins et Bastides en Côtes de Saint Mont" is a free brochure giving details (in French) of an offbeat itinerary that will acquaint you with its vineyards and winegrowers. For more information, tel. 05 62 69 62 87.

ACCOMMODATION

Château du Bascou,
Lieu dit Saint-Go,
32290 Bouzon-Gellenave.
Tel. 05 62 69 04 12.
Three guest rooms, each named for one of the region's varieties of vine, in a character-filled house at the heart of the vineyards. Enjoy hearty Gascon cuisine and wines in the evening at the *table d'hôte* of this couple of hotelier-winegrowers.

La Buscasse,
32400 Sarragachies.
Tel. 05 62 69 76 07.
A few miles from Riscle, this fine eighteenth-century wine-grower's residence offers three tastefully decorated guest rooms. There are sweeping panoramic views over the surrounding tree-filled estate and Saint-Mont vines.

RESTAURANTS

Château de Projan,
32400 Projan.
Tel. 05 62 09 46 21.
Located between Pau and Saint-Mont, this hotel-restaurant has taken up residence in a vast house with private estate on a hilltop. The décor is a successful mixture of elements drawn from various eras, and the sophisticated cuisine consists of regional dishes based around *foie gras*, *confit* (preserved duck), *magret* (duck breast), pigeon, and lamb.

La Bonne Auberge,
32370 Manciet.
Tel. 05 62 08 50 04.
After Nogaro on the road to Auch, this restaurant with its 1900s-style décor opens onto a typically Gascon village square. Sophisticated dining with copious portions of *piballes* (baby eels), pigeon, and raw *foie gras* with rock salt.

EVENTS

Last weekend in March: "Saint-Mont Vignoble en Fête." Tel. 05 62 69 62 87.

WINES

Producteurs Plaimont,
Chai de Saint-Mont.
Tel. 05 62 69 66 76.
Tastings and sale of good-value regional wines. The Château de Sabazan is mild and fruity; the Monastère de Saint-Mont is powerful and well-structured; and the Château Bascou is a good compromise between the two. As for the whites, Les Vignes Retrouvées is a fruity wine that is easy to drink, while the Tradition is typical of the appellation. As for Le Faîte, made in red and white, this is simply the finest Côtes de Saint-Mont. It is a selection of the finest barrels produced in the appellation, a blend created with the help of a panel of professional wine experts, *sommeliers*, and wine writers.

LANGUEDOC

COTEAUX DU LANGUEDOC

INFORMATION
Conseil Interprofessionnel des Vins du Languedoc (organization of Languedoc wineries),
6 place des Jacobins, BP 221,
11102 Narbonne.
Tel. 04 68 90 38 30.
www.languedoc-wines.com

ACCOMMODATION
Tourisme Vigneron.
Tel. 04 68 71 83 61.
A large network of winemakers able to provide comfortable accommodation for guests. Lodgings range from guest rooms to rural vacation cottage rentals.

La Chamberte,
rue de la source,
34420 Villeneuve-les-Béziers.
Tel. 04 67 39 84 83.
www.la-chamberte.com
You would be hard pressed to find anything more original than this converted *chai*. A timeless place, with a discreet décor and gastronomic *table d'hôte* that dishes up fresh, light menus using quality produce.

Château de Jonquières,
place de l'Église,
34725 Jonquières.
Tel. 04 67 96 62 58.
www.chateau-jonquières.com
Nestled against the Larzac plateau, this château in the heart of a village offers four spacious newly decorated guest rooms with their independent entrance, a summer lounge with pool table, and a refined dining room.

Hostellerie Cardabella,
10 place Fontaine,
34725 Saint Saturnin de Lucian.
Tel. 04 67 88 62 62.
A delightful inn in a leisurely setting on the main village square between the church and the *mairie*. Cozy rooms simply decorated and copious breakfast at very reasonable prices.

RESTAURANTS
Le Mimosa,
34725 Saint-Guiraud.
Tel. 04 67 96 67 96.
Is perfection to be found in a village of 240 souls? With a former dancer tending the stove and her husband,

a former violinist, playing waiter, the cuisine is a supple array of arabesques, and the wine list one of Languedoc's best. Exceptional value for money.

Auberge Saint-Martin,
11 avenue du Général de Gaulle,
34210 Beaufort.
Tel. 04 68 91 16 18.
This restaurant is set in the old village schoolhouse, but turn a blind eye to the décor and concentrate instead on the chef's unrivaled skill in fish specialties. Delicious lavender cream for dessert.

Le Tamarillos,
2 place du Marché aux Fleurs,
34000 Montpellier.
Tel. 04 67 60 06 00.
Trained under Guy Savoy and elected France's champion of desserts in 1985, Philippe Chapon proposes daring marriages of fruit and flowers with savory dishes, such as lightly fried *foie gras* and chocolate with compote of apples. For those looking for something different.

EVENTS
At Mas Saporta, on the second weekend in March, a hundred or so winemakers present their wines. there are also workshops for children and adults.

WINE MERCHANT
La Vieille Clairette du Languedoc,
7 place de la République,
34120 Pézenas.
Tel. 04 67 98 76 34.
Owner: Alain Reinaldos.

WINES
Château de Flaugergues,
1744 avenue Albert Einstein,
34000 Montpellier.
Tel. 04 99 52 66 37.
www.flaugergues.com
Owners:
Brigitte and Henri de Colbert.
This folly belongs to the descendants of Colbert, Louis XIV's famous controller of finances. Of the wines produced here, the Colbert is made from a blend of grapes from the best plots and is matured in barrels. The Sommelière is a pure expression of the *terroir* and is sufficient reason alone to visit this estate.

Château de l'Engarran,
34880 Lavérune.
Tel. 04 67 47 00 02.

www.chateau-engarran.com
Owner: Francine Grill.
No fewer than eleven different wines are made from the vines of this estate owned by three women. The pride of the house is the *vin de garde* known as Quetton Saint-Georges, which has an intense nose and opulent flavor with velvety tannins. The white Adélys develops notes of pear, honey, and citrus and is the perfect accompaniment to desserts based on tropical fruits.

Château Jonquières,
place de l'Eglise,
34725 Jonquières.
Tel. 04 67 96 62 58.
Owners: François and Isabelle de Cabissole.
This château, whose walls adjoin those of the village church, is proud of its horseshoe-shaped staircase and delightful guest rooms. Wines include an elegant red Barronnie, a blend of Syrah and Mourvèdre grapes, and a white made from an audacious blend of Grenache and Chenin known as Comte de Lausade.

Château de Montpezat,
route de Roujan, 34120 Pézenas.
Tel. 04 67 98 10 84.
www.chateau-montpezat.com
Owner: Christophe Blanc.
The success of this estate is due in part to its low yields. No more than three bunches are allowed to mature on each vine, producing highly concentrated wines such as La Pharaonne, a red based on 80 percent Mourvèdre, whose dark-berry flavor has opulence, power, and silkiness. Another red, Les Palombières, has an intense nose of black currant and spices. These are structured, powerful wines that exemplify what the appellation does best.

Le Mas de Saporta,
34970 Lattes.
Tel. 04 67 06 04 44.
www.coteaux-languedoc.com
This former winegrower's *mas*, dating from the seventeenth and eighteenth centuries, was refurbished to serve as a showcase for Coteaux du Languedoc wines. With its 250 wines and its restaurant, it is the ideal place to discover the appellation.

Prieuré Saint Jean de Bébian,
route de Nizas,
34120 Pézenas.
Tel. 04 67 98 13 60.
Owner: Chantal Lecouty.
While all the wines made by this wine writer are works of art, the white Prieuré is unquestionably among the finest white wines in the South of France. The red of the same name, which needs a good few years of bottle aging, is also remarkable.

Château Puech-Haut,
2250 route de Teyran,
34160 Saint Drézery.
Tel. 04 67 86 93 70.
The Prestige is one of the finest in the Languedoc. Vinified by famous wine expert Michel Rolland, it is fruity, supple, and subtle, and gives of its best when accompanying *magret de canard*. The white Tête de Cuvée has elegance and freshness, with buttery vanilla aromas.

Daumas Gassac,
34150 Aniane.
Tel. 04 67 57 88 45.
www.daumas-gassac.com
Owner: Aymé Guibert.
Daumas Gassac is one of the stars of the region, famous above all for its admirable red based on Cabernet Sauvignon, which needs many years of aging. The Terrasses range, made from traditional Languedoc varieties using grapes from a number of local growers, serves as a great introduction to the wines of the region.

MINERVOIS

INFORMATION
Syndicat d'Initiative de Minerve,
2 rue des Martyrs,
34200 Minerve.
Tel. 04 68 91 81 43.

Maison du Minervois,
Château de Siran,
34210 Siran.
Tel. 04 68 27 80 00.

Tourisme de Terroir,
Maison du Tourisme Vert,
78 ter rue Barbacane,
11000 Carcassonne.
Tel. 04 68 71 83 61.

Château de Violet,
Route de Pépieux,
11160 Peyriac-Minervois.
Tel. 04 68 78 10 42.
www.chateau-de-violet.com
A three-star hotel, restaurant, and wine estate, this château is a valuable find. The owner, a delightful elderly lady, welcomes guests as if they were part of the family.

Hôtel d'Alibert,
11160 Caunes, Minervois.
Tel. 04 68 78 00 54.
A hotel with seven guest rooms, run by a jovial music lover, in a Renaissance-style house set on the tiny square by the *mairie*. Highly commended regional cooking and wine list with a good Minervois selection.

La Barbacane,
Hôtel de la Cité,
place de l'Église,
11000 Carcassonne.
Tel. 04 68 71 98 71.
Luxurious guest rooms decorated in beige and white with views over the old city walls. Very stylish restaurant with blue and gold frescoes and wonderful wine list for those who demand the best.

RESTAURANTS
Mas Cambounet,
34150 Gignac.
Tel. 04 67 57 55 03.
Delicious organic cuisine vibrant with regional fare in a restored *mas* set on a wine and olive-growing estate. Small boutique selling olive oil and wine, and six-room vacation cottage with three-*épi* rating.

La Bastide de Cabezac,
18 hameau de Cabezac, 11120 Bize.
Tel. 04 68 46 66 10.
Fifteen minutes from Narbonne, this fine residence stands on the D5 known as "La Minervoise." Elegant restaurant with wine list featuring a score of Minervois labels. Twelve guest rooms, including two very spacious and airy suites with discreet, tasteful decoration.

Le Puits de Trésor, 21 rue Quatre Châteaux, 11600 Lastours.
Tel. 04 68 77 50 24.
Not far from Carcassonne and at the heart of the Orbiel Valley, Jean-Marc Boyer, who cut his teeth at the Ambroisie in Paris, dishes up the best the land and sea have to offer, using local produce. The *poulette du Cros* is not to be missed and there is also a fine regional wine list.

WINES
Château de Violet,
11160 Peyriac-Minervois.
Tel. 04 68 78 30 01.
www.chateau-de-violet.com
Owner: Emilie Faussié.
Recommended for its good-value, prize-winning Dame Blanche and Clovis. The little wine museum and charming boutique attached to the château are further reasons to visit.

Château Villerambert Julien,
11160 Caunes Minervois.
Tel. 04 68 78 00 01.
Owner: Michel Julien.
Although all three colors of wine are well made here, the laurels should go to the rosé, which is for people who do not like rosés. A deep salmon pink in color, it has aromas of strawberry, pomegranate, and sweet almonds with a spicy finish. It can be drunk throughout the meal and especially with spicy, exotic dishes.

Clos Centeilles, 34210 Siran.
Tel. 04 68 91 52 18.
www.clos-centeilles.fr
Owners: Daniel and Patricia Domergue.
One of the leading estates in the appellation, with wines that capture the expression of the grape and the *terroir*. Particularly attractive are the Capitelle de Centeilles, made from 100 percent Cinsault grapes, the Part des Anges, a spirited red the color of grenadine, and Carignanissime, a wine that will do much to prove wrong those who disparage the Carignan grape variety. The property also has a four-person *gîte* that is available for rent.

L'Ostal Cazes,
Tuilerie Basse,
34210 La Livinière.
Tel. 04 68 91 47 79.
Owner: Jean-Michel Cazes.
L'Ostal Caze is a delightful wine with a red and gold label inspired from the world of the circus. It is well-balanced and full-flavored.

Château Bassanel,
34210 Olonzac.
Tel. 04 68 27 27 00.
Owner: Jean Vezon.
Les Hauts de Bassanel, a wine that has won many medals, is the result of rigorous selection from the best plots and the oldest vines. The newest creation here is La Chapelle, which has a velvety garnet appearance and a delicious nose of red berries and the *garrigue*. It makes a superb accompaniment to shoulder of lamb or a mature Cantal cheese.

Château d'Oupia,
4 place du Château,
34210 Oupia.
Tel. 04 68 91 20 86.
Owner: André Iché.
The skillful André Iché makes good wines, including a magnificent rosé known as Emerantine and Nobilis, a red aged in new oak. One of the outstanding wines of the appellation in this windswept district.

COSTIÈRES DE NIMES

INFORMATION
Office de Tourisme de Nîmes,
6 rue Auguste, 30020 Nîmes.
Tel. 04 66 58 38 05.
www.ot-nimes.fr

ACCOMMODATION
Domaine des Clos,
route de Bellegarde,
30300 Beaucaire.
Tel. 04 66 01 14 61.
With its ideal situation on the "Route des Vins" (Wine Road), this eighteenth-century Provençal *mas* offers five guest rooms and seven charming vacation cottages, all wonderfully appointed. The welcome is as delightful as the homemade jams.

Domaine de la Fosse,
route de Sylvéréal,
30800 Saint-Gilles.
Tel. 04 66 87 05 05.
www.domaine-de-la-fosse.com
This former commandery founded by the Knights of Malta offers five guest rooms, decorated in a Camargue style. Swimming pool, sauna, hammam, and *table d'hôte*—paradise.

Château Mas Neuf,
Gallician,
30600 Vauvert.
Tel. 04 66 73 33 23.
www.chateaumasneuf.com
A former coaching inn on the Santiago de Compostela pilgrimage route, it was as renowned for the quality of its hospitality in the eighteenth century as it is today. Three comfortable, good-sized guest rooms with refined décor and vineyard views.

RESTAURANTS
L'Ex Aequo,
11 rue Bigot,
30000 Nîmes.
Tel. 04 66 21 71 96.
A floral, flower-bedecked setting around a vast patio with palm trees, yuccas, and oleander, just a couple of bull's horns away from the Nîmes arena. On the menu, frogs' legs tiramisu and veal rosette with fresh tuna mousse, all sprinkled with spices from the world over. Romantic or thoroughly modern, flowers add a touch of grace to each dish. Lavish wine list, as is only to be expected—the owner is an expert *sommelier*.

Chez Alexandre,
rue Xavier-Tronc,
Nîmes-Garons.
Tel. 04 66 70 08 99.
This restaurant just minutes from the airport is in a spruce red house with a terrace looking out on a garden with cedar trees. Michel Kayser, holder of a Michelin star, treats food lovers to *île flottante* with truffles on a cream of cepe soup, roast pigeon with licorice root, or *foie gras* with Jamaican pepper capsicum and black currant sauce.

WINES
Château de Valcombe,
Valcombe, 30510 Générac.
Tel. 04 66 01 32 20.
Owners:
Dominique and Bénédicte Ricome. Noteworthy for its Garance red, with a fresh, spicy nose and its Prestige. The latter is made from the oldest vines in the vineyard. It is a deep ebony purple in color with rich raspberry, mulberry, and violet aromas. Perfect for laying down.

Château Mourgues du Grès,
route de Bellegarde,
30300 Beaucaire.
Tel. 04 66 59 46 10.
www.mourguesdugres.com
Owners: François and Anne Collard.
There is plenty of talent and
attention to detail here, particularly
evident in the Capitelles rosé and
the red known as Terre d'Argence—
the finest wine in the appellation—
named in homage to the silver-leaved
alders on the estate.

Mas des Tourelles,
4294 route de Bellegarde,
30300 Beaucaire.
Tel. 04 66 59 19 72.
Owners: Hervé and Diane Durand.
Famous for its extraordinary Roman
wines—Mulsum, Turriculae, and
Carenum—and for its more sensual
Grande Cuvée, a blend of Syrah and
Mourvèdre from old vines. The latter
is a deep garnet red and has notes of
blueberry and pepper. La Cour des
Glycines, another blend from old
vines, is worth trying for its name
and wonderful structure.

Château de la Tuilerie,
route de Saint Gilles,
30900 Nîmes.
Tel. 04 66 70 07 52.
Owners:
Chantal and Pierre-Yves Comte.
The lovely tasting cellar here, called
Le Jardin des Vins (the Garden of
Wines), is stocked with tempting
flagons of wines with seductive
names such as Dîner de Chasse,
Bisous, Coup de Foudre, and Attrape
Cœur (adorned with a label
illustrated by Desclozeaux). The
château promises to donate twenty
cents from each bottle sold to the
P'tits Loups, a charity that helps
abused children.

Château d'Or et de Gueules,
chemin des Cassagnes,
route de Générac,
30800 Saint-Gilles.
Tel. 04 66 87 32 86.
Owner: Diane de Puymorin
The property has belonged to a
young woman, Diane de Puymorin,
since 1998. It makes three *primeur*
wines, another called La Bolida made
from Mourvèdre vines that are ninety
years old, and two late-harvested red
and white Vins de Pays d'Oc. All are
very well made.

Château Mas Neuf,
30600 Gallician.
Tel. 04 66 73 33 23.
Owner: Luc Baudet.
These wines have won many
gold and silver medals yet remain
very good value for money. The
Compostelle is the top wine, a red
matured in secondhand barrels. It
has a nose of dried figs, berries, and
nutmeg, developing as it ages into a
mixed-herb bouquet. It is ideal with
homemade *tapenade* (black olive
paste) or red meat. The white is
made from Roussanne and has notes
of furniture polish, honey, and
apricot jelly. It combines excellently
with seafood.

CORBIÈRES

INFORMATION
Office de Tourisme,
place Roger Salengro,
11110 Narbonne.
Tel. 04 68 65 15 60.

Maison des Terroirs,
Le Château, 11200 Boutenac.
Tel. 04 68 27 73 02.
A true showcase of the Corbières region's
wineries, the Maison des Terroirs is both
a *caviste* and an information center.
www.aoc-corbières.com

**Conseil Interprofessionnel des Vins
du Languedoc (organization of
Languedoc wineries),**
6 place des Jacobins,
11100 Narbonne.
Tel. 04 68 90 38 30.

ACCOMMODATION
Domaine du Haut-Gleon,
Villesèque-des-Corbières,
11360 Durban.
Tel. 04 68 48 85 95.
www.hautgleon.com
A fine wine grower's château offers six
guest rooms in its outhouses formerly
used by shepherds and grapepickers.
Suitably rustic-style furniture and
cheerful colors in the guest rooms.

La Mignoterie,
11220 Fajac-en-Val.
Tel. 04 68 79 71 42.
An attractive house not far from
Carcassonne, with four guest rooms
whose second hand furniture lends
a very personal touch to this
establishment, which has an

atmosphere half Surrealist and half
Baroque. A great place to stay.

Domaine de la Pierre Chaude,
Les Campets,
11490 Portel les Corbières.
Tel. 04 68 48 89 79.
www.lapierrechaude.com
Just fifteen minutes from the coast
and a sea-sprayed stone's throw from
the abbey of Fontfroide, this house
with its distinctive personality offers
two comfortable vacation cottages
and four guest rooms set around an
Andalusian-style patio.

RESTAURANTS
Auberge du Vieux Puits,
11360 Fontjoncouse.
Tel. 04 68 44 07 37.
With his modern cuisine using
traditional local fare, Gilles Goujon,
Meilleur ouvrier de France (Master
Artisan of France), is a chef whose
reputation and virtuosity reach
far beyond regional borders. A
gastronomic delight.

**Les Cuisiniers Vignerons
de l'Abbaye de Fontfroide.**
Tel. 04 68 41 86 06.
Less than ten miles from Narbonne,
in the exceptional setting of
this Cistercian abbey, simple
Mediterranean-style cuisine is the
order of the day. Open from March 1
to October 31.

WINES
Château de Luc,
11200 Luc-sur-Orbieu.
Tel. 04 68 27 10 80.
Owner: Louis Fabre.
The sweet wine known as Cuvée
des Etangs contains delightful notes
of *berlingot*, while the red Louis
Fabre de Luc has a nose of sour
cherries and licorice and a mouth
full of melting tannins.

Château Prieure Borde Rouge,
11220 Lagrasse.
Tel. 04 68 43 12 55.
Owners: Natacha and Alain
Devillers-Quenehen.
This is a popular address in
Corbières, best-known for its L'Ange,
Signature, and Jardin de Frédéric.
All reasonably priced, they offer
spicy, fruity flavors, fat tannins,
and a good finish. The property
also has two guest rooms, elegantly
decorated by the owner, who is a

former fashion designer who collects
angels. Mealtimes are lively.

Château Pech-Latt,
11220 Lagrasse.
Tel. 04 68 58 11 40.
Owner: Philippe Mathias.
His Sélection Vieilles Vignes red,
produced using biodynamic methods,
has been showered with honors.
His Alix, also a blend of grapes from
old vines, is another prizewinner.

Château la Baronne,
11700 Fontcouverte/Moux.
Tel. 04 68 43 90 07.
Owners:
Suzette and André Lignières.
This very romantic property, which
the owners bought as an engagement
present, produces particularly elegant
wines such as the Grenache en Vert,
with its lovely luminous color, lively
nose, and citrus fragrance.

Château Gleon Montanie,
11360 Durban.
Phone: 04 68 48 28 25.
www.gleon-montanie.com
Owners:
Jean-Pierre and Philippe Montanié.
The Gaston Bonnes is particularly
fine, with its marked nose of berries,
spices, and the Provençal *garrigue*.
This well-balanced wine is one of
the most popular of the appellation.
The owner is a former naval pilot.

Château Metairie des Joncs,
rue des Mimosas,
11360 Fontjoucouse.
Tel. 04 68 44 08 69.
www.mdesjoncs.com
Owners: Heidi and Ivan Puech.
The property is plain but endearing,
and the owners vinify organic wines
in all three colors. The results are
delicious and very reasonably priced,
with pretty and charmingly old-
fashioned labels.

ROUSSILLON

INFORMATION
**Conseil Interprofessionnel des Vins
du Roussillon (Organization of
Roussillon Wineries):**
19 avenue de Grande Bretagne,
66000 Perpignan.
Tel. 04 68 51 21 22.

Office de Tourisme,
Palais des Congrès, place Armand
Lanoux, 66000 Perpignan.
Tel. 04 68 66 30 30.

ACCOMMODATION
Park Hotel,
18 boulevard J. Bourrat,
66000 Perpignan.
Tel. 04 68 35 14 14.
This ideally situated Spanish-style
hotel provides a warm welcome and
also boasts Le Chapon Fin, the best
restaurant in town.

La Vieille Demeure,
6 rue du Llobet,
66400 Toreilles.
Tel. 04 68 28 45 71.
www.la-vieille-demeurs.com
A former sixteenth-century priory
with a fine cobbled patio surrounded
by orange and lemon trees. The
house, lovingly restored, has lost
none of its authenticity.

Hostellerie des Templiers,
quai de l'Amirauté,
66190 Collioure.
Tel. 04 68 98 31 10.
Over two thousand canvases signed
by great artists including Picasso,
Derain, and Matisse adorn the walls
of their former haunt. An institution.

RESTAURANTS
Al Fanal, Hôtel El Llagut,
18 avenue du Fontaulé,
66650 Banyuls sur Mer.
Tel. 04 68 88 00 81.
Restaurant with a nautical feel and a
sea view. Traditional fish-based fare,
superbly presented in southern-style
dishes.

La Littorine,
Hôtel Les Elmes, Plage des Elmes,
66650 Banyuls sur Mer.
Tel. 04 68 88 03 12.
Moored in a sandy creek, this
restaurant with its large picture
windows serves an original culinary
mix drawn from land and sea:
watermelon gazpacho with lobster,
fried *supions* (small cuttlefish) with
squid-ink pasta, roasted pig's knuckle
glazed with Banyuls. Enthusiasts of
the local wines will find over twenty-
eight different labels on the wine list.

Ferme-Auberge Les Clos de Paulilles,
route de Port-Vendres.
Tel. 04 68 98 07 58.

The romantic setting of the Bay of
Paulilles, where vine-covered slopes
sweep down gently to the sea, forms
the backdrop to a set menu that
pays homage to the wines of the
eponymous estate. Delights include
foie gras served with a Collioure
white, *escalivade* with a full-bodied
rosé, and compote of fruits on
chocolate cream accompanied by a
local wine, such as a sweet fortified
red *rimage*.

WINES
Mas Baux,
chemin du Mas Durand,
66140 Canet en Roussillon.
Tel. 04 68 80 25 04.
Owners:
Serge and Marie-Pierre Baux.
A handsome property making
immaculate Côtes-du-Roussillon and
Vins de Pays des Côtes Catalanes
with such provocative names as
Rouge à Lèvres (Lipstick), Rouge
Gorge (Robin Redbreast) and Beau
Blond (Handsome Blond). The
elegant silver labels have a useful a
thermometer symbol indicating the
ideal temperature at which the wine
should be drunk.

Domaine Cazes,
4 rue Francisco Ferrer,
66602 Rivesaltes.
Tel. 04 68 64 08 26.
Owners: André and Bernard Cazes.
Fifteen different wines ranging from
vins de pays to Côtes-du-Roussillon
and Côtes-du-Roussillon Villages, as
well as a Muscat de Rivesaltes. This
last one has an aromatic nose of
tropical fruits and very ripe grapes
and enhances the flavors of *foie gras*,
fruit tart, or sorbet.

Mas Amiel,
66460 Maury.
Phone: 04 68 29 01 01.
Owner: Olivier Decelle.
This very diverse range of wines
includes Muscat, Maury, *vins doux
naturels*, and Côtes-du-Roussillon
Villages. The Mas Amiel's Spéciale
10 Ans d'Âge deserves to be singled
out. With its nose of cocoa, stewed
prunes, fruit preserves, and spices,
it is the ideal accompaniment to
chocolate desserts, walnuts, and
coffee.

Domaine de Gauby,
1 carrer del Faratjal,
66600 Calce.
Tel. 04 68 64 35 19.
Owners: Gérard and Lionel Gauby .
This domaine, which uses
biodynamic methods, has attracted
accolades for its concentrated,
powerful wines. The Vieilles Vignes
is a *vin de pays*, which is smooth, full,
powerful, elegant, and very aromatic.
The red Les Calcinaires is a blend
from a *terroir* consisting of a seam of
limestone on schist. The yield is low
and the meticulous sorting of the
grapes results in a wine that is rich,
silky, and fruity, with perfect balance.
Truly a wine for connoisseurs.

Domaine de la Rectorie,
54 avenue du Puig del Mas,
66651 Banyuls sur Mer.
Tel. 04 68 81 02 94.
Owners: Marc and Thierry Parcé.
The Parcé family has been making
wine here for centuries. Their range
includes a Collioure rosé known as
La Goudie, which also exists in a red
version, and Banyuls such as Vin de
Pierre and l'Oriental.

Cellier des Templiers,
route du Mas Reig,
66650 Banyuls.
Tel. 04 68 98 36 91.
Superb and very representative
selection of the appellation. There is
no obligation to buy, just that of
tasting the wines. There are two fine
Banyuls *grands crus* called Cuvée
Président Vidal and Cuvée Amiral
Vilarem. The best white Collioure is
Madeloc and the best reds are the
Domaine du Roumani, Château des
Abelles, and the Abbaye de Valbonne.

Château de Jau,
66600 Cases de Pene.
Tel. 04 68 38 90 10.
Owner: Estelle Dauré.
This château is both a winemaking
venture, an art gallery, and a
restaurant, where the star of the show
is a little bistro wine called Le Jaja de
Jau. There are other fine wines with
sensual names like Talon Rouge
(Red Heel). The Côtes-du-Roussillon
Villages, a red with a deep color and
aromas of ripe fruits, also deserves a
mention.

Château de Caladroy,
66720 Bélesta.
Tel. 04 68 57 10 25.
Fax: 04 68 57 27 76.
The range called Les Schistes is made
up of attractive wines with notes of
dark berries and licorice, but perhaps
the most extraordinary wine here
is the the Rivesaltes Tuilé Grande
Réserve. It has a complex nose
of cherries, figs, and crushed
strawberries, fresh, spicy flavors, and
is sublime with ripe melon or fig tart.

Domaine du Clos des Fées,
69 rue du Maréchal Joffre,
6660 Vingrau.
Tel. 04 68 29 40 00.
Owner: Hervé Bizeul.
This former wine writer who
retrained as a winemaker is fanat-
ically demanding, so his wines are
top quality. His Petite Sibérie made
from Grenache has won many medals.

Domaine Saint-Roch,
66460 Maur.
Tel. 04 68 29 07 20.
Owners:
Emma and Marc Bournazeau.
This young couple, who live at the
foot of the Cathar Château de
Quéribus, produce white and red
vins de pays, Côtes-du-Roussillon
Villages, and dessert wines such as
the exceptional white Maury, which
has aromas of quince and pear.
Kerbuccio, a wonderful blend of
Mourvèdre, Grenache Noir, and
Carignan, also deserves a special
mention.

SOUTHERN CÔTES-DU-RHÔNE

CHÂTEAUNEUF-DU-PAPE

INFORMATION
Office de Tourisme,
place du Portail,
84230 Châteauneuf-du-Pape.
Tel. 04 90 83 71 08.

Maison des Vignerons,
12 avenue Louis Pasteur,
84230 Châteauneuf-du-Pape.
Tel. 04 90 83 72 21.
www.chateauneuf.com

ACCOMMODATION
Hôtel Les Fines Roches,
route de Sorgues,

84230 Châteauneuf-du-Pape.
Tel. 04 90 83 70 23.
This luxury hotel surrounded by vines should be a compulsory part of any romantic getaway. There are several dining rooms, including one in the library that could be straight out of the pages of a glossy interior design magazine. The cuisine is wonderfully fresh.

La Muscardine,
3 rue du Puits Neuf,
84230 Châteauneuf-du-Pape.
Tel. 04 90 83 53 86.
Owners: Yvon and Maryse Fournerie.
Charming guesthouse with a theatrical décor (the owner is a set designer). Spacious, comfortable rooms—be sure to ask for the blue room with four-poster bed.

RESTAURANTS
La Mère Germaine,
place de la Fontaine,
84230 Châteauneuf-du-Pape.
Tel. 04 90 83 54 37.
One room serves as wine bar and another is a gastronomic restaurant with a well-endorsed wine list. The place is a favorite haunt of celebrities, as can be seen from the array of photos on the walls. A warm welcome assured.

WINE MERCHANTS
La Bouteillerie du Palais des Papes,
Palais des Papes, 84000 Avignon.
Tel. 04 90 27 50 85.
The handsome firearms room of the Palais de Papes contains a tasting and sales room for the wines of the Côtes du Rhône. A total of forty wines have been selected by the experts on the tasting committee.

Vinadéa,
8 rue Maréchal Foch,
84230 Châteauneuf.
Tel. 04 90 83 70 69.
The wines of some ninety producers in the appellation are sold in this handsome vaulted cellar, at almost the same price as you would pay at the estate. Open daily, including Sundays and public holidays.
www.vinadea.com

WINES
Château Les Fines Roches,
1 avenue du Baron Leroy,
84230 Chateauneuf-du-Pape.
Tel. 04 90 83 73 10.
Owner: Robert Barrot.

Famous for its Henri Constantin cuvée with its spicy nose and elegant mouth with pleasant acidity, the wines of the château are vinified by the talented Gaëlle, daughter of the owner.

Château de Beaucastel,
84350 Courthézon.
Tel. 04 90 70 41 00.
Owners:
Jean-Pierre and François Perrin.
One of the leading estates of the appellation. The Vieilles Vignes, refined, exuberant, and aromatic expression of the Roussanne variety, is one of the finest white wines in France.

Château La Nerthe,
route de Sorgues,
84830 Châteauneuf-du-Pape.
Tel. 04 90 83 70 11.
Owner: Alain Dugas.
This is one of the most sought after estates of the appellation, particularly popular with the Michelin-starred restaurants owned by such celebrity chefs as Alain Ducasse and Michel Bras, who have long displayed it on their wines lists. The red Les Cadettes and the white Clos de Beauvenir are particularly fine, but need to be left for a few years in a cellar.

Château Fortia,
route d'Avignon,
84230 Châteauneuf-du-Pape.
Tel. 04 90 83 72 25.
This 75-acre (30-hectare) estate belongs to the descendants of Baron Le Roy, instigator of the whole concept of the Appellation d'Origine Contrôlée. Wines are vinified in the traditional manner here, giving them great elegance and authenticity. They are also excellent value for money.

Domaine de la Solitude,
route de Bédarrides,
84230 Châteauneuf-du-Pape.
Tel. 04 90 83 71 45.
Owner: Jean Lançon.
An excellent range includes the Barberini, a blend from the best plots on the estate that goes well with duck or red meats, and the powerful, velvety Réserve Secrète, which has notes of spices and coffee and goes well with a chocolate dessert or a clafoutis.

CÔTES-DU-RHÔNE VILLAGES

INFORMATION
Office de Tourisme,
place du Marché,
84190 Beaumes de Venise.
Tel. 04 90 62 94 39.

Maison des Vins, 6 rue des Trois Faucons, 84000 Avignon.
Tel. 04 90 27 24 00.
www.vins-rhône.com

ACCOMMODATION
Château de Massillan,
Hauteville, 84100 Uchaux.
Tel. 04 90 40 64 51.
www.chateau-de-masillan.com
The present owners, a couple of designers, have given a new bloom of youth to the former residence of Diane de Poitiers by turning it into a hotel. Its twelve guest rooms are fully furnished in a sober, contemporary style. Prepare for a treat—this is an idyllic choice for a weekend away.

Le Grand Jardin,
84190 Lafare.
Tel. 04 90 62 97 93.
At the heart of the Dentelles de Montmirail on the Beaumes de Venise side, this hotel's ten Provençal guest rooms occupy a row of small terraced cottages. Each room has a patio overlooking the vines against the rugged backdrop of the Dentelles.

RESTAURANTS
Restaurant Côté Sud,
84100 Uchaux.
Tel. 04 90 40 66 08.
The former chef of the Epuisette in Marseille has found a new lease on life in this restaurant decorated with sea grass. The food is colorful, light, and tasty.

Le Grand Pré,
Roaix, 84110 Vaison-La-Romaine.
Tel. 04 90 46 18 12.
On the outskirts of the village, this smart establishment with a southern twist is run by a German and a Mexican *sommelière*. A small fountain and shady terrace grace the outside, while inside all is pure lines of white and wood. Exceptional wine list.

WINE MERCHANTS
Le Palais du Vin,
RN7, 84100 Orange.
Tel. 04 90 11 50 00.

A magnificent setting containing six hundred different wines in a gigantic cellar with a restaurant.

WINES
Château Saint Estève d'Uchaux,
route de Sérignan,
84100 Uchaux.
Tel. 04 90 40 62 38.
Fax: 04 90 40 63 49.
Owners: Thérèse and Marc Français.
This is an estate for lovers of both wine and classical music, because concerts are performed on the terrace of the château. As for the wines, these are Côtes-du-Rhône and Côtes-du-Rhône Villages. There are some magnificent and original whites based on Viognier, including the Thérèse, a rich, complex wine of which only 2,600 bottles are made annually. Among the reds, the full-bodied Grande Réserve is particularly attractive, with its black currant and truffle flavors.

Domaine de la Renjarde,
route d'Uchaux,
84830 Sérignan-du-Comtat.
Tel. 04 90 83 70 11.
Owner: Alain Degas.
This estate stands on the remains of a Roman town and belongs to the owner of the Château La Nerthe in Châteauneuf-du-Pape. The wines here are structured, velvety, and rounded, with flavors of ripe fruits and sweet spices, as illustrated by its Réserve de Cassagne.

Domaine de Mourchon,
La Grande Montagne,
84110 Séguret.
Tel. 04 90 46 70 30.
Owner: Walter McKinley.
This estate may be miles from anywhere, but it's certainly worth a detour. The cellar is right up to date and the wines elegant—and vice versa. The Grande Réserve and Tradition should be drunk with winter dishes in sauce and strong cheeses.

GIGONDAS

INFORMATION
Office de Tourisme de Gigondas,
place du Portail,
84190 Gigondas.
Tel. 04 90 65 82 46.

Inter Rhône,
6 rue des Trois Faucons,
84000 Avignon.
Tel. 04 90 27 24 00.
www.vins-rhone.com

ACCOMMODATION
Les Florets, 84190 Gigondas.
Tel. 04 90 65 85 01.
Nestling in a pretty pine grove at the heart of the Dentelles de Montmirail are these thirteen two-star guest rooms and a rustic inn-style restaurant. Diners can enjoy delicious Provençal cuisine served in elegant crockery on a terrace with stunning views.

RESTAURANTS
Restaurant l'Oustalet,
place du village,
84190 Gigondas.
Tel. 04 90 65 85 30.
Set on the picturesque village square, the house of Gabriel Meffre, wine merchant and producer, offers light refined Provençal cuisine.

Le Moulin à Huile,
quai Maréchal Foch,
84110 Vaison la Romaine.
Tel. 04 90 36 20 67.
In this old millhouse with ocher walls and blue shutters by the Roman bridge, Robert Bardot, *Meilleur ouvrier de France* (Master Artisan of France), lovingly creates Provençal flavors with a hint of India: Serrano ham chips, lobster *boudin* sausage, and Tandoori-style lamb. There are tree guest rooms, where decorative wrought iron makes for a truly Provençal atmosphere.

THINGS TO DO
Cave de Cairanne,
route de Bollène,
84290 Cairanne.
Tel. 04 90 30 82 05.
The Cairanne cooperative at the foot of the Dentelles has orchestrated a novel concept in sensory journeys with a stimulating introduction to wine tasting.

WINES
Château de Saint-Cosme,
84190 Gigondas.
Tel. 04 90 65 80 80.
Owner: Louis Barruol
One of the best estates in the appellation. Wines are matured in oak barrels, giving them a more contemporary touch.

Château Raspail,
84190 Gigondas.
Tel. 04 90 65 88 93.
Owner: Christian Meffre.
Eugène Raspail, nephew of the French politician for whom boulevard Raspail in Paris is named, built this lovely residence in 1866. The reds are found in the finest restaurants in the *département*.

Domaine des Tourelles,
84190 Gigondas.
Tel. 04 90 65 86 98.
Owner: Roger Cuillerat.
The seventeenth-century mansion was the first house to be built outside the village walls. The residence, which has a bell tower, is surrounded by vines and receives visitors in its huge eighteenth-century subterranean cellar that opens into two impressive vaulted chambers.

VACQUEYRAS

INFORMATION
Syndicat d'Initiative,
place de la Mairie,
84190 Vacqueyras.
Tel. 04 90 12 39 02.

Maison des Vignerons,
84190 Vacqueyras.
Tel. 04 90 65 88 37.

ACCOMMODATION
Domaine de la Ponche,
84190 Vacqueyras.
Tel. 04 90 65 85 21.
A château dating from 1629, now an elegant guesthouse run by a Swiss couple, offers a mellow atmosphere full of charm. The six individual guest rooms, including one suite with its own fireplace, exude an *art de vivre* that is quintessentially Provençal. Be sure to ask for the turret room.

RESTAURANTS
La Bastide Bleue,
route de Sablet,
84110 Séguret.
Tel. 04 90 46 83 43.
A typical *mas* with blue shutters offers eight Provençal-style guest rooms, as well as wholesome southern cooking served on a shady terrace in summer.

Auberge de Cabasse,
route de Sablet,
84110 Séguret.
Tel. 04 90 46 91 12.
A wine estate, three-star hotel, and restaurant, the Auberge de Cabasse is a haven of peace at the foot of one of France's most beautiful listed villages. On offer, twelve guest rooms and traditional Provençal cuisine with vegetables from the estate's kitchen garden.

EVENTS
Early June: Concours des Vins Jury-Consommateurs, Vacqueyras. This competition offers wine enthusiasts the opportunity of offering their opinions on the wines of the Rhône valley. All the members of the jury are amateurs.
Mid-July: Fête des Vins. This the oldest wine festival in the Rhône valley and includes all of its wines. There is a huge meal for eight hundred people and the day ends with a *bal populaire*.

WINES
Domaine la Fourmone,
route de Bollène,
84190 Vacqueyras.
Tel. 04 90 65 86 05.
Owners:
Aline and Marie-Thérèse Combe.
La Fourmone's white Fleurantine, a blend of Clairette and Grenache, is delightful. The nose is dominated by fresh floral and fruity notes, and the flavor is wonderfully harmonious.

Château de Montmirail,
cours Stassart,
84190 Vacqueyras.
Tel. 04 90 65 86 72.
Owner:
Monique Archimbaud-Bouteiller.
Of the five wines made here, special mention should be made of the Saint-Gabriel, a white wine that goes well with seafood, and L'Ermite, a red with spicy aromas, and powerful, tannic flavor that goes well with pâtés, game, and cheeses.

Domaine de Montvac,
84190 Vacqueyras.
Tel. 04 90 65 85 51.
Owner: Jean and Cécile Dusser. Cécile, daughter of Jean, is a delightful winemaker who originally wanted to be a dancer. Her wines do

indeed dance, being fresh and graceful, as well as being excellent value for money.

Les Christins: Perrin & Fils.
This wine is available at the Château de Beaucastel and the Repaire de Bacchus. Vinified by the famous Château Beaucastel at Châteauneuf-du-Pape, it has fragrances of leather and amber. Buy with confidence.

CÔTES-DU-VENTOUX

INFORMATION
Syndicat Général des Vignerons (Union of Wine Growers),
Château Durbesson,
route de Velleron,
84200 Carpentras.
Tel. 04 90 63 36 50.
www.cotes-ventoux.com

Office de Tourisme,
Hôtel Dieu, place Aristide Briand,
84200 Carpentras.
Tel. 04 90 63 00 78.
www.provenceguide.com

ACCOMMODATION
Château Talaud,
84870 Loriol-du-Comtat.
Tel. 04 90 65 71 00.
www.chateautalaud.com
In the former eighteenth-century estate of the Marquis Grille l'Estoublen, a charming Dutch couple offer six spacious guest rooms furnished with fine antiques, and lavish breakfasts. This is an exceptional address on the outskirts of Avignon.

L'Aube Safran,
chemin du Patifiage,
84330 Le Barroux.
Tel. 04 90 62 66 91.
François, an architect, and Marie, a talented interior designer, are the owners of this guesthouse that offers four rooms. With its old-style plasterwork and whitewash, all is organic and homespun—a success in terms of both style and hospitality. The *table d'hôte* is based around fresh produce and homegrown saffron. A real treat.

La Bastide de Voulonne,
84220 Cabrières d'Avignon.
Tel. 04 90 76 77 55.

www.bastide-voulonne.com
An old Provençal country house decked with fabrics and soft furnishings in cheerful hues to dispel the blues. A calm, comfortable, and convivial paradise close to Gordes. Fresh market-style cuisine.

RESTAURANTS

Le Saule Pleureur,
145 chemin de Beauregard,
84170 Monteux.
Tel. 04 90 62 01 35.
Not to be missed for lovers of truffles. Michel Philibert brings out the very best in them with panache. A gastronomic delight.

Le Vert Galant,
12 rue de Clapies, Carpentras.
Tel. 04 90 60 20 15.
Although the restaurant's décor may have seen better days, Michel Castelain is a full-fledged member of the truffle brotherhood. Say no more. Lavish set menus in which *noisette* of lamb in pastry stir-fried with cepes and chayote squash competes with braised lobster in mild spices.

VINEYARD TOURS

The tourist office offers tours of the vineyard starting from Carpentras. The tour takes the D13 toward Caromb, then from Crillon le Brave it continues toward Bédoin and takes the D213 to Flassan, with its red ocher frontages. It then proceeds along the D150, stopping at Mazan to taste the Sautel sweet wine, before returning to Carpentras.

WINES

Château Unang,
route de Méthamis,
84570 Malemort du Comtat.
Tel. 04 90 69 91 37.
www.chateauunang.com
Owner: James King.
This vineyard in the heart of the Gorges de la Nesque, a protected site of outstanding natural beauty, surrounds one of the oldest châteaux in the Vaucluse. It produces reds, whites, and rosés.

Château Pesquié,
route de Flassan - BP6,
84570 Mormoiron.
Tel. 04 90 61 94 08.
www.chateaupesquie.com
Owners: Paul and Edith Chaudière.
The finest wine here is the red

Quintessence, made only in the best years using selected grapes from the oldest vines. Its velvety texture and flavor of berries and vanilla make it one of the greatest Côtes du Ventoux. The delightful Terre Précieuse is deliciously fruity and balanced.

Domaine de Fondrèche,
84380 Mazan.
Tel. 04 90 69 61 42.
Owners: Sébastien Vincenti and Nanou Barthélémy.
Their Persia is made with 90 percent Syrah matured in vats. It is soft in the mouth with subtle tannins. The Blanche has an aromatic nose of vanilla and fresh almonds.

Domaine Brusset,
84290 Cairanne.
Tel. 04 90 30 82 16.
The estate is well known for its Cairanne and Gigondas. Boudale is a Côte du Ventoux with a dark ruby color and a nose of cherry and blueberry, mixed with a note of resin, black olives, and cloves. It's a wonderful accompaniment to red meat.

CÔTES-DU-LUBÉRON

INFORMATION

Vaucluse Tourist Board,
12 rue Collège-de-la-Croix,
84008 Avignon.
Tel. 04 90 80 47 00.

Syndicat Général des Vignerons (Union of Wine Growers),
90 boulevard Saint-Roch,
84240 La Tour d'Aigues.
Tel. 04 90 07 34 40.

ACCOMMODATION

L'Auberge de l'Aiguebrun,
Domaine de la Tour, D943,
84480 Bonnieux.
Tel. 04 90 04 47 00.
This timeless place in the heart of the Lubéron National Park is a mellow and stylish haven of calm. Delicious traditional cuisine. A meditative paradise.

La Bastide de Marie,
route de Bonnieux,
84560 Ménerbes.
Tel. 04 90 72 30 20.
www.c-h-m.com
A voluptuous oasis of luxury in the form of an eighteenth-century *mas*,

providing an intimate romantic refuge for the happy few. Treat yourself (and your partner) to an unforgettable experience.

Domaine de la Tuilière,
chemin Tuilière,
84160 Cadenet.
Tel. 04 90 68 24 45.
In a superb eighteenth-century country house surrounded by a wine estate covering thirty acres (twelve hectares), this captivating guesthouse offers five guest rooms and already has a loyal following.

GÎTES GARNIS

(vacation rentals and more)
Each guest room is provided with literature on Luberon wines, as well as a bottle of a local wine in an initiative to help the visitor discover what the region has to offer. More information from the Syndicat des Vignerons des Côtes du Lubéron:
Tel. 04 90 07 34 40.

RESTAURANTS

La Fenière,
Campagne Bellevue,
route de Lourmarin,
84160 Cadenet.
Tel. 04 90 68 11 79.
Surrounded by the *garrigue* and lavender fields, this handsome residence's main draw is Reine Sammut's cooking. Simplicity and southern talent are the main ingredients in the cuisine of this accomplished chef. The fish and vegetable dishes are superb. Some guest rooms also available.

Le Fournil,
5 place Carnot,
84480 Bonnieux.
Tel. 04 90 75 83 62.
Guy and Jean Christophe fell under the spell of this terrace with its hundred-year-old plane trees. They have created a contemporary bistro in a grotto, and provide attentive service in a relaxed atmosphere. The menu features market produce cooked in fine Provençal style. Reservations essential.

La Maison Gouin,
RN100, Coustellet,
84660 Maubec.
Tel. 04 90 76 90 18.
Wonderfully fresh and stylish Provençal cuisine. The wine list with

no restaurant mark up is a den of discovery, and diners even fetch their own bottle from the cellar. Best to make reservations, given the popularity of the place.

EXPLORING THE VINEYARDS

Two footpaths take you through vineyards containing explanatory notices about the wines, grape varieties, and *terroirs*. Each walk lasts around one and a half hours. One starts at the Terrasses de Sainte-Cécile at the village of Oppède. The other starts at the cooperative at Cucuron.

WINES

Château La Canorgue,
Jean-Pierre Margan,
route du Pont-Julien,
84480 Bonnieux.
Tel. 04 90 75 82 98.
The owner of this estate has won many gold medals and has been voted best winemaker of the year for the entire Rhône valley. Produced organically, his wines are balanced, voluptuous, and complex. They include a fruity, elegant Blanc de Blancs, made from Clairette and Bourboulenc, that is the finest in the appellation.

Domaine de la Citadelle,
84480 Ménerbes.
Tel. 04 90 72 41 58.
Owner: Yves Rousset-Rouard.
This former film producer has made a successful transition into winemaking. The wine-tasting area, with its corkscrew museum and attractive boutique, should not be missed. The Gouverneur is a magnificent wine, concentrated yet refined, made from the best plots of the estate. His Vin de Pays de Vaucluse, made from Viognier, has a wonderful flavor of peaches and apricots.

Domaine de Marie,
route de Bonnieux,
84560 Ménerbes.
Tel. 04 90 72 54 24.
Owners:
Jocelyne and Jean-Louis Sibuet.
The "Le" is the most irresistible wine here. The elegant bottles and the tasting-room are worth seeing.

Val Joanis,
route de Cavaillon,
84120 Pertuis.

Tel. 04 90 79 20 77.
Owners: Jacques and Cécile Chancel.
The location is beautiful and the
wines, particularly those of the
Les Griottes range, delicious.
The red, recommended by Robert
Parker, has notes of licorice,
black-berry, and prune, and toasty
flavors of spices and vanilla.
The magnificent gardens are open
to the public and the tastingroom
includes a boutique selling lovely
items for the home.

Château de Mille,
84440 Apt.
Tel. 04 90 74 11 94.
Owner: Conrad Pinatel.
The oldest vineyard in Lubéron
is well worth visiting. The robust,
vigorous red has a temperament
as authentically local as that of
the owner. A true wine for keeping
and a testament to the *terroir*.

PROVENCE AND CORSICA

BANDOL

INFORMATION
**Comité Départemental du Tourisme
du Var,**
1 boulevard Foch,
83003 Draguignan.
Tel. 04 94 50 55 65.
www.tourismevar.com

ACCOMMODATION
Domaine de Frégate,
83270 Saint-Cyr-sur-Mer.
Tel. 04 94 32 57 57.
Nestling among the vines, this four-
star establishment by the sea exudes
southern color. From its windows
and the terrace of its restaurant, you
can enjoy a full view of one of the
region's finest golf courses. There are
133 rooms, three outdoor terraced
swimming pools, and a restaurant
that serves the estate's own wines.
A place not to be missed.

RESTAURANT
Hostellerie Bérard,
rue Gabriel Péri,
83740 La Cadière d'Azur.
Tel. 04 55 33 16 55.
This restaurant is set on the hillside
of one of the region's most beautiful
villages and has spectacular views.
The dishes showcase local produce.

Thirty-seven three-star guest rooms
allow you to linger longer over the
view.

EVENTS
First Sunday in September: Fête des
Vendanges at La Cadière d'Azur.
First Sunday in December: Fête du
Millésime in Bandol.

WINES
Château de Pibarnon,
83740 La Cadière d'Azur.
Tel. 04 94 90 12 73.
Owner: Comte Henri de Saint-Victor.
The wines of Château de Pibarnon
set the standard for Bandol and
regularly win at wine tastings. Inded,
they have now established themselves
among the best wines in France.
The red, which is 90 percent
Mourvèdre, has wonderful depth and
balance and an aromatic power of
rare intensity.

Domaine de Frégate,
route de Bandol,
83270 Saint Cyr sur Mer.
Tel. 04 94 32 57 57.
The estate is next door to a four-star
hotel and grows the Mourvèdre and
Grenache red varieties that produce
structured, virile, powerful wines
with a nose of violets and mulberries
that develops as it ages into notes of
undergrowth. The dry, fresh Blanc de
Blancs makes a wonderful aperitif
and the fruity rosé is delicious.

Château Romassan,
Domaines d'Ott,
601 route des Mourvèdres,
83330 Le Castellet.
Tel. 04 94 98 71 91.
www.domaines-ott.com
The estate is famous for its rosés,
regarded by some as the finest in the
world. The Cœur de Grain wine is
magnificent with a Chinese or Indian
meal. As for the Cuvée Marine, it
goes extremely well with sashimi or
any other seafood, though purists
would drink it as an aperitif.

Château Vannières,
83740 La Cadière d'Azur.
Tel. 04 94 90 08 08.
Owner: Eric Boisseaux.
Winner of numerous medals,
this is the wine by which all other
Bandols are judged. Reds, whites,
and rosés are vinified in the finest
tradition of the appellation, and a

Vin de Pays du Mont-Caume is also
made. For the reds, the grapes are
hand-picked and vinified in oak vats
to create round, silky wines that can
be laid down for between ten and
twenty years.

BAUX DE PROVENCE

INFORMATION
**Office de Tourisme des Baux
de Provence,**
rue Porte Mage,
13520 Les Baux de Provence.
Tel. 04 90 54 34 39.

ACCOMMODATION
L'Oustau de Baumanière,
chemin départemental 27,
13520 Les Baux de Provence.
Tel. 04 90 54 33 07.
Jean André Charial's handsome
residence is part of the Relais et
Châteaux network and boasts two
Michelin stars. Superb guest rooms
recently refurbished by a famous
interior designer.

Le Prince Noir,
13520 Les Baux de Provence.
Tel. 04 90 54 39 57.
This artist's residence is a timeless
place perched in the highest house
in the village. Vast panoramic
terrace covering 1,615 square feet
(150 square meters), and the kind
of stylish comfort one wishes could
be found everywhere.

Jas de l'Ange,
route d'Eygalières,
13660 Orgon.
Tel. 04 90 73 39 50.
Simply paradise. The region's finest
guesthouse with a swimming pool
reminiscent of a pond set in a
verdant meadow. There is also a
medieval kitchen garden overlooked
by one beautifully appointed room
set apart. Light lunches served.

RESTAURANTS
L'Assiette de Marie,
1 rue Jaume Roux,
13210 Saint-Rémy de Provence.
Tel. 04 90 92 32 14.
The "thrift store" style décor is the
biggest draw. Nothing matches—the
plates, glasses, and chairs all having
been gleaned from various sources—
but the overall effect is one of
harmony. On the menu: fresh pasta

and Provençal-style stuffed
vegetables.

Le Parc des Cordes,
chemin départemental 17,
13990 Fontvieille.
Tel. 04 90 54 67 85.
In the depths of the *garrigue* at the
heart of the Alpilles, this small
family-style establishment has a
convivial atmosphere and offers good
value for money. Tiny *tellines* (Venus-
shell clams) available on Saturdays
when in season.

Le Garde Manger,
13103 Saint-Etienne du Grés.
Tel. 04 90 49 08 37.
Discreet crockery and bold cuisine
in this simple old stone-built
restaurant. Cepe ravioli with
shavings of mature Gouda,
poultry supreme with morels.
The wine list features mainly small
local producers and offers very good
value for money.

WINES
Château Romanin,
13210 Saint-Rémy de Provence.
Tel. 04 90 92 45 87.
www.romanin.com
The red Le Cœur de Romarin
encapsulates the essence of the *terroir*
and is a classic example of winemaking skills. Each new addition to
this range, started in 1998, bears a
different name and is produced in
limited quantities: Primus (1998)
was produced in only 900 bottles;
Quartus (2001) in 8,000 bottles.
The red, white, and rosé La Chapelle
de Romanin, all made from young
vines, are also delicious.

Domaine de Trévallon,
13103 Saint-Etienne du Grès.
Tel. 04 90 49 06 00.
Owners: Eloi and Floriane Dürrbach.
Although not part of the appellation
of Les Baux de Provence, the
winemaker, a former architecture
student, now produces the most
highly regarded *vin de pays* in France,
under the label of Vin de Pays des
Bouches-du-Rhône. His unusual
blend of Cabernet Sauvignon and
Syrah produces a wine that is fine,
structured, and powerful, with a nose
that is marked by the *garrigue* and
red berries. As for the white, it gives
off aromas of honey and verbena.
Extraordinary.

Domaine de Terres Blanches,
route de Cavaillon,
13210 Saint-Rémy de Provence.
Te: 04 90 95 91 66.
Owner: Guillaume Rerolle.
The Aurélia red made here is a wine
for laying down with a shining ruby
color and complex bouquet of
garrigue, spices, smokiness, and sour
cherries. It is blended from Cabernet
Sauvignon, Syrah, and Grenache.
The rosé is equally exciting, one
of the best in the appellation.

Mas de la Dame,
13520 Les Baux de Provence.
Tel. 04 90 54 32 24.
Owners: Anne Poniatowski and
Caroline Missoffe.
This, the leading winemaking and
olive oil-making estate in the region,
is run by two women who work
together to produce wonderful wines,
such as the Du Vallon des Amants,
which is structured and powerful,
and Le Coin Caché, an elegant
red based on overripe Vieux
Grenache with a nose of cassis.
As for the white of the same
name, it has a nose of brioche
and toast and is the ideal companion
to chicken.

Château d'Estoublon,
route de Maussane,
13990 Fontvieille.
Tel. 04 90 54 64 00.
Owners: Rémy and Valérie Reboul.
This ancient château houses a
grocery store in which wonderful
flavors and superb olive oils are
on display, including local honey
and spices. There are also a number
of interesting wines very attractively
labeled. These include a ruby
red with very dense fragrances
of cherry and peony with a very
full, round mouth and a very
voluptuous and lively white whose
flavors develop into hazelnut,
butter, and pineapple.

COTEAUX D'AIX-EN-PROVENCE

INFORMATION
**Comité Départemental
du Tourisme du Var,**
1 boulevard Maréchal Foch,
83003 Draguignan.
Tel. 04 94 50 55 50.

Office de Tourisme,
2 place du Général de Gaulle,
13100 Aix-en-Provence.
Tel. 04 42 16 11 61.
www.coteaud'aixenprovence.com

ACCOMMODATION
La Bastide du Cours,
43 cours Mirabeau,
13100 Aix-en-Provence.
Tel. 04 42 26 10 06.
www.bastideducours.com
Five guest rooms that celebrate the
painters of Aix and provide a trip
back to the time of Napoleon III and
the libertine eighteenth century, with
candlelit dinners in the Directoire
room or the more glamorous
Renaissance-style lounge.

La Canestelle,
quartier Cabanes, chemin rural 24,
13610 Le Puy Sainte Réparade.
Tel. 04 42 61 86 60.
Set in an atmospheric house in large
grounds, three immaculate guest
rooms with brightly colored walls
adorned with *boutis* embroidery and
patchworks open directly onto the
garden with swimming pool. The
owner, an avid *boutis* embroiderer,
offers her guests lessons in this
Provençal needle art.

RESTAURANTS
Relais Sainte-Victoire,
13100 Beaurecueil.
Tel. 04 42 66 94 98.
At the foot of Mont Sainte-Victoire,
René Bergès serves fresh cuisine
based on regional produce in a spruce
room with light wood trim or on the
delightful terrace in summer. Menu
changes monthly. Warm welcome.

L'Amphitryon,
2 rue Paul Doumer,
13100 Aix-en-Provence.
Tel. 04 42 26 54 10.
Restaurant full of urban chic and
painted in warm hues. With its
antique furniture, publicity posters
on the walls, and colorful seating, it
is authentically Provençal and dishes
up fresh and original market-style
cuisine. A flavorsome address.

WINES
Château Revelette,
13490 Jouques.
Tel. 04 42 63 75 43.
Owner: Peter Fischer.
This estate, whose vineyards lie

behind Mont Sainte-Victoire, makes
some attractive reds, whites, and
rosés that are best drunk when they
are young and fruity. The red Grand
Vin shows true potential for keeping
and has aromas of berries and spices
allied to good structure.

Château Bas,
13116 Vernègues.
Tel. 04 90 59 13 16.
Owner: Georges de Blanquet.
Château Bas is built on a Gallo-
Roman citadel and deserves more
than one visit. Of the nine wines
produced here, the best are the red,
white, and rosé of the Cuvée du
Temple range (in homage to the
lovely monument in the grounds of
the estate). The red is particularly
good, with silky tannins and intense
red berry flavors.

Domaine de Fonscolombe,
13610 Le Puy-Sainte-Réparade.
Tel. 04 42 61 70 00.
www.fonscolombe.com
This château produces mostly rosé
wine, together with some red and
a small amount of white. Both
the Cuvée Spéciale and the Cuvée
Gourmande are available in all
three colors. The château itself is a
handsome building dating from the
early eighteenth century.

CÔTES-DE-PROVENCE

INFORMATION
Comité Départemental du Var,
1 boulevard Maréchal Foch,
83003 Draguignan.
Tel. 04 94 50 55 50.

**Office de Tourisme
de la Provence Verte,**
83170 Brignoles.
Tel. 04 94 72 04 21.

Maison des Vins,
RN 7, 83460 Les Arcs.
Tel. 04 94 99 50 10.
www.cotes-de-provence.fr

ACCOMMODATION
Château de Berne,
Flayosc, 83510 Lorgues.
Tel. 04 94 60 43 60.
www.chateauberne.com
A four-star hotel set in 1,600 acres
(650 hectares) of nature and vines.
The luxurious house offers thirteen

guest rooms and six comfortable
suites, most of which have their own
fully functional fireplace. Concerts,
recitals, and jazz evenings are
organized, as well as lessons in wine
and Provençal cuisine.

Hôtel Juana,
La Pinède, avenue Gallice,
06160 Juan les Pins.
Tel. 04 93 61 08 70.
www.hotel-juana.com
This hotel, with its Art Deco
architecture completely refurbished
1930s style, boasts a famous restaurant,
La Terrasse, which has a remarkable
wine list. The ideal address for a perfect
match of victuals and wine.

La Villa Marie,
chemin Val Rian, 83350 Ramatuelle.
Tel. 04 94 97 40 22.
www.c-h-m.com
Overlooking the Bay of Pampelone,
this most recent addition to the
Sibuet family hotels has a lot to offer.
The guest rooms favor unbleached
linen, cheesecloth, and terra-cotta
hues. Shellfish and seafood are the
main culinary delights.

RESTAURANTS
Chez Bruno,
Campagne Mariette,
83510 Lorgues.
Tel. 04 94 85 93 93.
In his grandparents' house, this
renowned truffle expert—who gets
through around six tons a year—has
Provence wrapped around his little
fork. Truffles are everywhere: on
gnocchi, potatoes, crayfish, and
scrambled eggs. There are a few guest
rooms with colorful walls adorned
with Provençal *boutis* embroidery to
appeal to romantics.

Le Moulin de Mougins,
Notre-Dame de Vie,
06250 Mougins.
Tel. 04 93 75 78 24.
Everyone (who is anyone) was
familiar with this old sixteenth-
century oil mill, the former preserve
of Roger Vergé who knew how to
attract talent and beautiful people to
his restaurant. Alain Llorca, former
chef at the Negresco in Nice, is the
new owner. The weekday lunch
menu represents very good value for
money.

DISCOVERING THE WINES

Château Sainte Roseline,
83460 Les-Arcs-sur-Argens.
Tel. 04 94 99 50 30.
www.sainte-roseline.com
Owners:
Françoise and Bernard Teillaud.
The Prieuré wines come in three
colors and are produced from low-
yielding vines on the best plots. As
befits wines of this name (meaning
"priory"), they should be drunk with
reverence.

Château de Saint-Martin,
route des Arcs,
83460 Taradeau.
Tel. 04 94 99 76 76.
Owner: Adeline de Barry.
Although all the wines on the
estate are vinified to the same high
standard, the Comtesse de Saint-
Martin range is outstanding,
consisting of a red, white, and rosé
made from a selection of grapes
from old vines. As for the red
Grande Réserve, it is smooth and
concentrated, as refined as a *grand cru*.

Clos Mireille,
route du Fort de Brégançon,
83250 La Londe-les-Maures.
Tel. 04 94 01 53 53.
www.domains-ott.com
The Clos Mireille is one of the three
estates belonging to the Domaines
Ott. Here the vines run right down
to the beach, giving the white wines
great expressiveness. There is a dry
Blanc de Blancs that is supple and
has a complex nose of fruits and
sweet spices and a Blanc de Côte of
great freshness and subtlety, full of
the fragrances of white flowers. The
wine is a wonderful companion to
Provençal cooking and goat cheese.

Château Roubine,
RD562, route des Vins,
83510 Lorgues.
Tel. 04 94 85 94 94.
www.chateau-roubine.com
Owners:
Valérie and Philippe Riboud.
This *cru classé* belongs to the former
Olympic fencing champion Phillipe
Riboud. The labels are designed by
artists, adding to the charm of the
wines. The rosé is based on Tibouren,
the southern variety par excellence,
and leaves a hint of apricot in the
mouth, mixed with the citrus flavors
that go so well with scallops and
stuffed vegetables. The white wine
has a note of honey and butter
combined with white flowers and
wood, highlighting the flavors of
spicy foods and fish cooked in sauce.

Château Rasque,
83460 Taradeau.
Tel. 04 94 99 52 20.
Owners:
Monique and Gérard Biancone.
The Alexandra comes in magnums of
white and rosé in frosted glass bottles
that would cause a sensation at a
formal dinner table. The wines are
refined and have delicious fragrances.
There is a superb tasting room in
hacienda-style and the main driveway
is lined with vines each labeled with
details of the variety, a true initiation
into wines and winemaking.

Château de Léoube,
route de Léoube,
83230 Bormes-les-Misosas.
Tel. 04 94 64 80 03.
Its magnificent red Les Forts de
Léoube is made from the oldest vines
on the estate. The exceptional rosé,
made from grapes harvested when
ripe, is carefully vinified by Romain
Ott, a member of the famous Ott
family of winemakers.

CORSICA

INFORMATION
Office de Tourisme Corse,
3 boulevard Roi Jérôme,
20181 Ajaccio, Corsica.
Tel. 04 95 51 53 03.

**Comité Interprofessionnel
des Vins Corses (organization
of Corsican wineries),**
7 boulevard du Général de Gaulle,
place Saint-Nicolas,
20200 Bastia, Corsica.
Tel. 04 95 32 91 32.

ACCOMMODATION
Château Calvello,
20253 Patrimonio.
Tel. 04 95 37 01 15.
Three very well appointed spacious
guest rooms in a sixteenth-century
feudal château overlooking vineyards.
Highly tasteful décor, warm
welcome, and very good value for
money.

Hôtel Bellevue,
20217 Saint Florent.
Tel. 04 95 37 00 06.
www.bellevue.com.fr
The blue and white color scheme of
this nineteenth-century establishment
has a distinctly Greek feel. The guest
rooms have four-poster beds with
mosquito netting and the bar is of
polished zinc. For romantics at heart.

RESTAURANTS
U Scogliu,
Marine de Cannelle,
20217 Canari.
Tel. 04 95 37 80 06.
You need to negotiate a number of
dizzying hairpin bends, while trying
not to be distracted by the sight of the
sea in the background, to reach this
little cottage, which is located in the
depths of a creek in Cap Corse, the
northern tip of the island. Marie-José
and Christian Leonetti's specialties
are shellfish, seafood, and fish in salt
pastry. Absolutely delicious. An
address worth noting.

Le Belvédère,
route plage de Palombaggia,
20137 Porto Vecchio.
Tel. 04 95 70 54 13.
With its traditional architecture, this
hotel, set in a grove of eucalyptus,
pines, and palms on the beach facing
the old town of Porto Vecchio, gives
pride of place to regional products,
with such delights as roast Corsican
veal and scampi ravioli. The extensive
wine list allows you to select the
perfect match for your meal.

A Casarella,
6 rue Sainte-Croix,
20200 Bastia.
Tel. 04 95 32 02 32.
This place is set in the heart of
the Citadel with a superb terrace
overlooking the old port. The daring
chef has perked up traditional
Corsican dishes with original
lightness. On the menu: sardine
fritters with Corsican *brocciu* cheese,
Bastia-style anchovies, and veal cutlet
rolls with herbs, all washed down
with local wines. Reservations
recommended.

WINES
Clos Landry,
carrefour de l'Aéroport,
20260 Calvi.
Tel. 04 95 65 04 25.
Owners: Fabien and Cathy Paolini.
AOC Calvi wines have been made
here for four generations. They
include a *rosé gris* that is supple, full,
lively, and floral, with notes of wood
and licorice. A classic.

Clos d'Alzeto,
20151 Sari d'Orcino.
Tel. 04 95 52 24 67.
Owners: Albertini Frères & Fils.
The highest estate on the island
produces classic wines, including two
well-balanced reds: Prestige and
Tradition. The rosé is acidic with
complex flavors and is the ideal wine
to accompany a Provençal meal.

Clos Canarelli,
Tarabucetta,
20114 Figari.
Tel. 04 95 71 07 55.
Owner: Yves Canarelli.
Nature expresses itself freely here in
one of the most promising vineyards
of the appellation. Clos Canarelli
makes reds, whites, and rosés. The
white is particularly fine, with a
luminous yellow color, a nose of
lavender, bay leaf, and eucalyptus,
and great freshness in the mouth.

Clos Capitoro,
20166 Porticcio.
Tel. 04 95 25 19 61.
Owner: Jacques Bianchetti-Pisciatella.
The distinctive labels of this estate
with its walled vineyards bear a bull's
head. Reds, whites, and rosés are
produced here. The red, which needs
bottle aging, has a licorice aroma and
goes wonderfully with red meats. The
sparkling *méthode champenoise* blanc
de blancs, the Impérial Cyrnos, is
unique in the region.

Domaine Orenga de Gaffory,
20253 Patrimonio.
Tel. 04 95 37 14 25.
Owner: Henri Orenga de Gaffory.
This is perhaps the most modern
winemaking operation on the island,
as well as being a center for
contemporary art and a delightful
store. Try the refined Muscat, with
intense honey and citrus aromas. The
red Cuvée des Gouverneurs of the
AOC Patrimonio has great potential
for laying down, developing delicious
aromas of preserved fruits as it ages.

PHOTO CREDITS

2	Christian Sarramon
4	Christian Sarramon
6–7	Paul Palau
8	Guillaume de Laubier
11	Christian Sarramon
12–13	Jean-Luc Barde/Scope
15	Jean-Luc Barde/Scope
16 (left)	Christian Sarramon
16 (right)	Jean-Luc Barde/Scope
17	Jean-Luc Barde/Scope
18–19	Jean-Luc Barde/Scope
20	Christian Sarramon
21	Château du Cayrou, David Nakache
23	Christian Sarramon
24	Domaine Salettes
25	Christian Sarramon
26–27	Repérant/Explorer
28	Domaine Saurs
29	Guillaume de Laubier
31	Guillaume de Laubier
32–33	Guillaume de Laubier
34	Guillaume de Laubier
35	Christian Sarramon
36	Alain Alquier
37	Christian Sarramon
39	Christian Sarramon
40	Alain Alquier
41	Christian Sarramon
42–43	Paul Palau
45	Paul Palau
46–47	Paul Palau
48–49	Paul Palau
51	Paul Palau
52	Paul Palau
53	Christian Sarramon
54	Guillaume de Laubier
55	Christian Sarramon
56	Paul Palau
58–59	Paul Palau
60 (left)	Paul Palau

60 (right)	Christian Sarramon
61	Château Villerambert Julien
63	Jean-Luc Barde/Scope
64	Paul Palau
65 (left)	Mas Neuf, photo Lionel Flusin
65 (right)	Christian Sarramon
66	Mas Neuf, photo Lionel Flusin
67	Château Simone, photo Camille Moirenc
69	Noël Hautemanière/Scope
70	Paul Palau
72	Christian Sarramon
73	Noël Hautemanière/Scope
74–75	Paul Palau
77	Paul Palau
78	Christian Sarramon
79 (left)	Paul Palau
79 (right)	Christian Sarramon
80–81	Guillaume de Laubier
82	Christian Sarramon
83	Christian Sarramon
84	Jean-Luc Barde/Scope
85 (left)	Christian Sarramon
85 (right)	Paul Palau
86	Noël Hautemanière/Scope
87	Paul Palau
88–89	Jacques Guillard/Scope
91	Christian Sarramon
93	Jacques Guillard/Scope
94	Jacques Guillard/Scope
95	Jacques Guillard/Scope
96	Gérard Sioen
97 (left)	Christian Sarramon
97 (right)	Christian Sarramon
99	Christian Sarramon
100–101	Jacques Guillard/Scope
103	Christian Sarramon
104	Jacques Guillard/Scope
105	Domaine de Cabosse, Photo Eliophot, Aix-en-Provence

107	Laurent Giraudou/Terra
108–109	Jacques Guillard/Scope
111	Christian Sarramon
112	Christian Sarramon
113	Laurent Giraudou/Terra
115	Christian Sarramon
116	Guillaume de Laubier
117	Christian Sarramon
118–119	Christian Sarramon
120	Jacques Guillard/Scope
121	Christian Sarramon
122–123	Jacques Guillard/Scope
125	Jacques Guillard/Scope
126–127	Jacques Guillard/Scope
128–129	Christian Sarramon
130 (left)	Jean-Luc Barde/Scope
130 (right)	Christian Sarramon
131	Jacques Guillard/Scope
133	Jean-Luc Barde/Scope
134–135	Jean-Luc Barde/Scope
136	Christian Sarramon
137	Jacques Guillard/Scope
139	Jacques Guillard/Scope
140	Château Simone, photo Camille Moirenc
141	Château Simone, photo Camille Moirenc
142–143	Jacques Guillard/Scope
145	Domaines Ott, Clos Mireille
146	Christian Sarramon
147	Jacques Guillard/Scope
148	Jacques Guillard/Scope
149	Christian Sarramon
150–151	Christian Sarramon
153	Christian Sarramon
155	Jean-Luc Barde/Scope
156	Roland Huitel/Scope
157 (left)	Jean-Luc Barde/Scope
157 (right)	Jean-Luc Barde/Scope
158–159	Jean-Luc Barde/Scope
160	Guillaume de Laubier

ACKNOWLEDGMENTS

The author warmly thanks the following for their assistance, valuable
support, and encouragement:
Olivier Renoir who watches over my life as over a precious vintage,
Donatien my little boy, for his joie de vivre and his outlook on life that has
changed my own; Lucie Guinat, my grandmother, for her sparkling humor
and gaiety; Gisou Bavoillot for her valuable advice and confidence; Nathalie
Demoulin for her sweetness and her great respect for authors; Sylvie Ramaut
for her infectious good humor; Christine Ontivéro for her organizational
skills; Marie Gaudel for her availability, kindness, and professionalism;
Sophie Janvier for her reliability and her friendship that passes every test;
Sophie Morgaud for her efficiency and generosity; Sylvie Boczkowski
and Inter-Rhône for their quickness to act; Maurice Bouchet for his daily
benevolence; Caroline Allain for having invited me into her home;
Fabienne Labeyrie for her loyal friendship and generosity; Yolaine de la Bigne
for her bubbly spirit and her smile; Daniel Llose for having given me some
valuable lessons in humility; Marion Ott for her spontaneous kindness;
Françoise and Bernard Teillaud for having welcomed me with open arms;
Antigone and Jean-Luc Schilling for the treasures they were kind enough to
let me taste; and Valérie Cassou, my childhood friend who departed forever
a mere hour after our last meeting.

And also:
Martine Albertin, Fabienne Amiach, Amélie and Gaëlle Barrot, Adeline
de Barry, Patrick Basset, Isabelle Blin, Françoise Boucher, Jack Burlot,
Jean-Michel Cazes, Pascal Chevrot, Estelle Dauré, Sonia Delagrange,
Guillaume de Laubier, Mélanie Degoua, Perrine Dequecker, André Dubosc,
Stéphane Gambier, managing director of Hôtel & Lodge, Marie Catherine
Gault, Jean Philippe Granier, Eric and Dominique Hernandez, Françoise
and Antonio Hernandez, Catherine Sick, Valérie Kéréver, Michelle Piron-
Soulat, Serge Latil, Dannie Launay, Brigitte Lurton and Jean Marc Isabelle
Maurin, Jean-Pierre Margan, Mauricette Mordan, Dominique Ventura,
Henri and Monique Parrat, Christian Sarramon, Maggy Maillet for her
enthusiasm, Mick Gerriet-Mahé, Asli Gensiray, Marie Segal,
Geneviève Renard, Dominique and Marie Odile Massenez, Mireille Brun,
Delphine Rousseau, France Bigoudan, Carole Hernandez, Pierre Fabre,
Claude and Marie Renard, Martine Tartour, Sylvie Prieur, Jacques Boscary,
Simone and Jean François Lefevère, François and Muriel Mallet,
Brigitte Saubesty, Greg and Johanne de Lepinay, Isabelle Revel,
Françoise Boucher, Catherine Bourdelin, Annie Ligen, François Millau,
Dominique Schiavi, Marie Catherine Gault, Anne Granclément,
Chantal Lecouty, Chantal Comte, Edna and André Degon, Alain Jessua
and Régine Magne, Delphine Rousseau, Julien Fournier, Manuel and
Françoise Mesquita, Michel Blanc, Michel Portos, and Nelly Vaillot.

Translated from the French by Josephine Bacon
Copyediting: Bernard Wooding
Typesetting: Claude Olivier-Four
Proofreading: Chrisoula Petridis
Color Separation: Penez Éditions, Lille

Distributed in North America by Rizzoli International
Publications, Inc.

Simultaneously published in French as *Vins du Soleil*
© Éditions Flammarion, 2005
English-language edition
© Éditions Flammarion, 2005

www.editions.flammarion.com

05 06 07 4 3 2 1

FC0474-05-III
ISBN: 2-0803-0474-7
EAN: 9782080304742
Dépôt légal: 03/2005

Printed in Italy by Canale